UNDERGROUND
ART

Please take your litter home

 You may have noticed that for the time being all litter bins have been removed from the Underground. Now more than ever we need your help to keep the trains and stations tidy and safe.

Please take all your litter home with you.

First published in Great Britain in 1990

Second edition published in 2001
by Laurence King Publishing
an imprint of Calmann & King Ltd
71 Great Russell Street
London WCIB 3BP
Tel: + 44 20 7430 8850
Fax: + 44 20 7430 8880
e-mail: enquiries@calmann-king.co.uk
www.laurence-king.com

Design © 2001 Calmann & King Ltd
Text © 2001 Transport for London

This book was designed and produced by Calmann and King
Ltd, London, in association with London's Transport Museum

A catalogue record for this book is available
from the British Library.

ISBN 1 85669 242 6

Design: Karen Stafford

Printed in Singapore

Front cover: Richard Spice: PLEASE TAKE YOUR LITTER HOME,
1991 (detail)
Back cover: E. M. Dinkel: THE WEST-END IS AWAKENING,
1931 (detail)

ACKNOWLEDGEMENTS

The revival of interest by London Transport in commissioning artworks for
new posters, which took place in the mid-1980s, was one of the main
prompts that led me to work on the first edition of this book in 1989. At
that time I had just left the London Transport Museum to pursue my
museum career outside London. After twelve years managing local authority
museum services in Colchester, Poole and Buckinghamshire I returned to
Covent Garden in a new capacity as Head of Collections for the retitled
London's Transport Museum. I rejoined the Museum in April 2001 soon after
being asked to provide this revised and updated edition of Underground
Art, which takes the poster story into the new Millennium.

Fortunately the intervening years have seen a continuing enthusiasm for
posters and a sustained recognition that high standards of design are an
important feature of the transport business. The quality of posters and
related publicity work for the Underground and buses today is a dramatic
improvement on the situation twenty years ago.

I would like to reiterate my thanks to everyone who provided assistance and
encouragement in the preparation of the first edition of Underground Art,
particularly Andrew Scott, Paul Castle and Jonathan Riddell of the London
Transport Museum. Julia Engelhart and Nicholas Dorman assisted in the
research on artists. Michael Levey and Dr Henry Fitzhugh were immensely
helpful in explaining poster commissioning policy. Julia Holberry typed the
manuscript and made many valuable editorial suggestions. Jane Havell of
Calmann & King was an ideal editor. For assistance with the second edition
my further thanks go to Sheila Taylor, Jonathan Riddell, Michael Walton and
David Ellis at the Museum and Philip Cooper at Calmann & King.

The poster archive at London's Transport Museum, which contains over
5000 posters, has been copied on to a digital database, which is available for
consultation in the Museum's Learning Centre. Further information on the
posters is also available on request (Tel: 020 7379 6344). Reproductions of
historic posters and copies of contemporary posters are available from the
Museum Shop.

Oliver Green
May 2001

OLIVER GREEN

UNDERGROUND ART

LONDON TRANSPORT POSTERS 1908 TO THE PRESENT

 LAURENCE KING

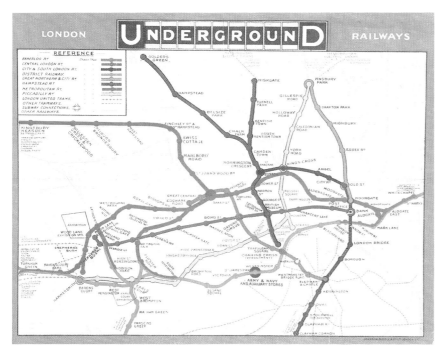

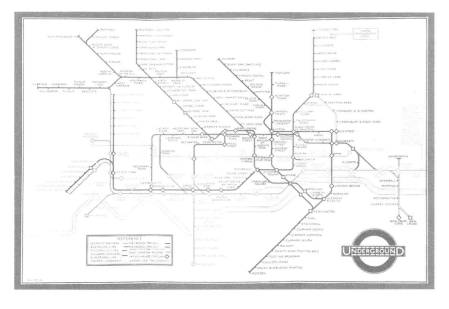

When the first Underground maps appeared in 1908, the system was sufficiently compact to be represented easily with geographical accuracy. As extensions were added in the 1920s, it became increasingly difficult to fit the whole Underground system on one map. In 1931, Henry C. Beck (1903–74), a young draughtsman working for the Underground, came up with a radical solution to the problem. In his spare time Beck had redesigned the map as a diagram, completely abandoning geographical accuracy for the sake of clarity. His layout, apparently inspired by diagrams of electrical circuits, showed the various lines as verticals, horizontals and 45-degree diagonals. The central area, which contained the most complicated interchanges, was enlarged in relation to the outer areas, making the map much easier to read.

Beck's unsolicited idea was tested by the Underground in 1933, initially as a folding pocket map, and was an instant success with passengers. He continued to experiment with, and adapt, his design until the late 1950s, but these and all subsequent versions of the diagram remain true to his original concept. It has inspired numerous imitations: the diagrammatic map is now a standard means of representing transport systems all over the world.

A POSTER TRADITION

THE PICTORIAL POSTER IS A VISUAL TELEGRAM, a concise means of conveying a message through a simple combination of words and images. At its best it is also an art form, albeit an applied art where the designer's skill and creativity is channelled towards a very practical purpose. The poster's function may be to sell a product or a service, to explain or to persuade. It may be used as advertising, publicity or pure propaganda. In any of these fields it can be a powerful means of communication which is difficult to ignore. A well-designed poster will attract attention and transmit an idea almost before the viewer has had time to think about it.

The modern poster is little more than a century old, the product of a growing mass market for consumer goods and services that developed towards the end of the nineteenth century. Improvements in printing techniques and reproduction methods made the pictorial colour lithographic poster a suitably cheap and effective medium for advertising and publicity. It came into widespread use in the 1890s and 1900s, but it was not until the 1920s and 1930s that the mass-produced poster reached a peak of stylistic quality. This was very much the golden age of poster design, before the advent of other more direct advertising media which have tended to overshadow it since the 1950s. Popular colour magazines, radio and, above all, television have progressively left the poster with a secondary supportive role, although the best contemporary designs can still have a striking impact.

London Transport and its immediate predecessor, the Underground Group of companies, have a well-founded reputation for the quality of their advertising and publicity. No other comparable organization has made such consistent and sustained use of pictorial posters, or maintained such high standards of design. The posters reproduced in this book are a representative selection from over three thousand originals held in the London Transport Museum's archives. They span more than eighty years and reveal a very wide range of artistic styles, constituting a cross-section of British graphic

design in this century. The posters also document the remarkable way in which one organization successfully developed this particular publicity medium as a corporate image for its entire operation.

LONDON'S TRANSPORT

London in 1900 was the largest city in the world. In the course of the previous century its population had increased from just under one million to some six and a half million inhabitants, and the urban area had spread rapidly in every direction. This growth was closely associated with the development of public transport, which allowed people to live in suburbs some distance from their place of work. On the roads a network of bus routes had been growing since the 1830s, supplemented after 1870 by tram services on the main roads out into the suburbs. Suburban railway services had also developed rapidly since the middle years of the century, allowing longer distance commuting than the buses and trams. These railways included the first two underground lines, the Metropolitan and the District, which ran mainly in covered cuttings in the built-up central areas of London, but were soon extended overground into the suburbs and beyond. Further suburban development often followed in the wake of the railway, and many of the villages in the countryside around London became engulfed in the growing metropolis.

Dramatic technological changes took place in all forms of urban transport in the early years of the new century. Victorian transport was almost totally reliant on the horse and steam locomotive as sources of motive power. In the Edwardian era this situation changed very quickly. The first regular motor-bus service in London was introduced in 1899; only fifteen years later the last horse-bus was withdrawn. Electric trams appeared in 1901 and had replaced every horse-tram in the capital by 1915. Mechanized buses and trams were larger than their horse-drawn predecessors and could be operated over greater distances, allowing more passengers to be carried over much longer routes.

Until 1890 all London's railways, including the two underground lines, used steam locomotives. The opening of the City and South London Railway in 1890 offered a revolutionary alternative: it was the first electric underground railway in the world, running in deep-level tunnels with a circular profile – hence the name 'tube'. By 1907 six more

electric tube railways had opened under London, and the two original steam underground railways, the Metropolitan and District, had been largely electrified.

These developments in transport technology were accompanied by new organizational structures. Building electric tramways and underground railways was expensive, and many companies found it difficult to raise the enormous capital sums required. One large private company, the Underground Electric Railways of London Ltd, quickly came to dominate the urban transport scene. The UERL was set up in 1902 by an American financier, Charles Tyson Yerkes, who had a somewhat shady background in tramway promotion in Chicago. Using the UERL as a holding company, Yerkes planned to buy up and modernize tramways and railways throughout London. He died in 1906 before all his ambitions had been fulfilled, but his organization continued to grow. Yerkes already had a controlling interest in the District Railway, and in the space of less than a decade the UERL proceeded to take over three tramway companies, the main London bus company and two existing tube railways, as well as completing the construction of three new tube lines. By 1914 the Underground Group, as the UERL and its subsidiaries became known, was the major operator in London.

The successful consolidation of the Underground Group was by no means a smooth passage. The strong American influences in the organization, from Yerkes' principal financial backers to the engineering methods and electrical equipment used, made it a natural target for criticism in the chauvinistic British press. This was compounded by the Underground's initially poor financial performance. When the three new UERL tube railways opened in 1906–7 none of them carried anything like the number of passengers that the company had confidently anticipated.

The turnround in the company's fortunes followed the appointment of a new General Manager, Albert Stanley, who joined the London Underground from the New Jersey Tramways in 1907. Stanley was not American (he had emigrated from England with his family at an early age), but his transport career had been made entirely in the United States. He brought to the Underground a dynamic American management style which had an almost immediate impact on the company. Within a few months of his arrival, he called a meeting of his principal officers and announced that the company faced bankruptcy if it continued on its existing course. All those present were asked to hand in their resignations, which would take effect after six months if financial returns had not improved. In the event, no resignations were required, because within that time the company's performance did improve – dramatically. This story was told many years later by Stanley himself in a press interview and may be an elaboration of the facts, but it is a revealing anecdote about the man who was to bring about the unification of London's transport services. Stanley, later Lord Ashfield, was subsequently made Chairman and Managing Director of the UERL, and from 1933 was the first Chairman of the new London Passenger Transport Board.

FRANK PICK'S PUBLICITY DRIVE

Improving the Underground's rather poor public image was an essential part of the recovery process, and it was here that a young man called Frank Pick made his first significant contribution. Pick, born in 1878 in Spalding, Lincolnshire, qualified as a solicitor in 1902 and joined the traffic statistics office of the North Eastern Railway as a management trainee in the same year. Later he became personal assistant to the General Manager, Sir George Gibb, in the company's head office at York. When Gibb was appointed Deputy Chairman and Managing Director of the Underground Group in 1906, he brought the 28-year-old Pick to London with him. Shortly after Stanley's arrival, Pick was transferred to the new General Manager's office, and early in 1908 was given responsibility for the Underground Group's publicity. It was a field in which he had no experience, and for which he had no apparent qualifications. Trained as a lawyer and statistician, he had no background in art or advertising. He had, however, been highly critical of the Underground's early attempts at

Frank Pick (1878–1941): his passionate interest in design included many areas outside his career as a transport manager. He was a founder-member of the Design and Industries Association, which was formed in 1915 to encourage better standards of commercial and industrial design, and became its President in 1932. In 1934 he was the first Chairman of the Council for Art and Industry, forerunner of the present Design Council.

Posters promoting the bus services first appeared after the Underground Group's takeover of the London General Omnibus Company in 1913. They were often produced in the smaller double crown size (30 × 20 in.) for display on the front panels of the open-top vehicles, as shown here with a 1913 poster for Hatfield by Charles Sharland.

publicity, and Stanley now gave him the opportunity to see if he could do better. It was to prove a far-sighted decision.

The early publicity that appeared when the three new tube lines opened in 1906–7 was quite extensive, and in some areas showed an imaginative approach by the Underground's passenger agent Walter Gott. There were press announcements, leaflets about each line, and free folding pocket-maps showing the whole system. All these ideas were useful, but they lacked the impact of a planned and coherent programme that could pull together the company's various activities and establish a positive corporate image in the minds of the public. Pick saw the opportunity to do this through posters, an advertising medium which had initially been conceived largely as a means of raising revenue by charging *other* companies for poster space on stations. The Underground used very few posters to publicize its own activities, and when it did they were traditional 'letterpress' productions with no pictorial content.

At this time some of the more progressive main-line railway companies were already using coloured lithographic posters for publicity purposes, not least Pick's own former employer, the North Eastern, which promoted Scarborough and other seaside resorts that were served by its trains. Pick took the same technique and adapted it to London, carefully cultivating the notion that everything the great city had to offer was available through travel by bus, tram or Underground, which in turn were portrayed as the very lifeblood of the capital. It was a brilliant advertising concept, although Pick was the first to admit that the success of the poster publicity campaign was not achieved overnight, nor with any clear idea at the outset of how it might develop. Pick's biographer quotes a characteristically modest comment he made much later in life: 'After many fumbling experiments I arrived at some notion of what poster advertising ought to be. Everyone seemed to be quite pleased with what I did and I got a reputation that really sprang out of nothing.'

The earliest Underground posters were commissioned from printing firms who usually employed their own or freelance commercial artists to produce the original artwork, which was then translated into poster form by the firm's lithographers. Pick's initial 'fumbling experiments' were not so much concerned with the production techniques as with the way in which the Underground used its posters. He recognized the importance of presentation, and the need to reorganize the chaotic mass of advertising and information that covered the walls of so many railway stations at the turn of the century. It was an unattractive and inefficient system: passengers found it difficult to pick out basic information about services, or even station names, while advertisers were

The 'winged wheel' device, used on the side panels of the London General Omnibus Company's new motor buses from 1905. The same device was featured on the cap badges of the bus crews when staff uniforms were introduced a few years later.

competing for more and more space in a mad scramble which did little to promote their particular product.

Pick reserved special illuminated boards at the Underground station entrances for the company's own pictorial posters and maps. Commercial advertising displays were confined to the walls of the platforms and passages inside the stations, and were restricted to carefully delineated grids, which could also include an allocation of space for the Underground's own use. The poster grids on the station platforms were separated from the station nameboards which, after 1908, appeared in an early version of the bar and circle symbol with the station name in white on a blue bar across a red disc.

The typography of the posters also required special attention. Pick was not happy with the traditional typefaces used by the printers, and decided that the Underground needed its own display typeface to distinguish the company's information clearly from the other commercial advertising on its property. The eminent calligrapher Edward Johnston was

The original Underground Bill Store in 1908, two years after it had been opened in a room above Hammersmith station in West London. It was run by one man with a boy to assist him: the 'boy' shown in this picture was A.E. Fruin, who began working for the company in 1906. The photograph was kindly provided by his grandson Trevor Davey, who also worked for the London Underground.

ABCDEFGHIJKLMNOPQRSTUVWXYZ
abcdefghijklmnopqrstuvwxyz
1234567890£!/?.,''():;--c%

The Johnston Typeface ...

The sans serif display alphabet designed for the Underground in 1916 by calligrapher Edward Johnston (1872–1944) was a major advance in typography. Pick wanted a design with 'the bold simplicity of the authentic lettering of the finest periods', and yet 'belonging unmistakably to the twentieth century'. Johnston had made a detailed study of early letter forms, and met Pick's requirements by turning to classical Roman capitals for his inspiration and proportions. Once these had been established the alphabet, he claimed, 'designed itself'. It is based on squares and circles, Johnston's O being a perfect circle and his capital M a square with the diagonal strokes meeting exactly in the centre of the letter.

The Johnston typeface was a copyright design for the exclusive use of the Underground Group, but imitations soon followed at home and abroad. Its major progeny in Britain was Gill Sans, designed by artist–craftsman Eric Gill (1882–1940) for the Monotype Corporation in 1928. Gill Sans was adopted by the London and North Eastern Railway for all its signing, and the lettering soon became a standard printer's typeface throughout the industry. Gill had been a pupil of Johnston, and freely acknowledged that his own much better-known typeface was in fact a close variant on Johnston's classic Underground design.

For comparison, both Johnston and Gill Sans have been used in this book. Headings and chapter introductions are in New Johnston, the slightly amended version used by the Underground since 1979. The remaining text is in Gill Sans: Johnston, being a display typeface, is not really suitable for small-scale use.

... and Gill Sans

commissioned to design the new lettering and produced his first version of it in 1916. Johnston's classic Underground typeface is based on plain, carefully proportioned block letters where the main strokes are of equal thickness and there are no end strokes or serifs. It is ideal for use on posters and signs where clarity and legibility at a distance are essential. The Underground has used it for nearly all its display signing since the 1920s and a modified version known as 'New Johnston' is still the standard typeface applied to the Underground's posters today.

Pick rarely used posters for direct, 'hard sell' advertising. Even in the early days, when the main purpose of the publicity was to build up traffic levels on the underused system, the approach was usually to entice the prospective traveller indirectly. The posters only rarely showed the *method* of travel, and concentrated mainly on the destination. Once the habit of travelling regularly by bus or Underground had been established, it was less essential to advertise season tickets or business travel; commuters and other rush-hour travellers were by then a captive market and did not need to be told about their everyday experience. On the other hand, they and their families could be encouraged to make extra journeys in off-peak periods such as evenings and weekends, when many of the Underground Group's trains and buses were otherwise lying idle. Most of the posters were therefore gentle inducements to leisure travel, a large proportion featuring destinations in London's countryside. After the takeover of the London General Omnibus Company in 1913, the Underground Group could offer a growing range of rural excursions, often with a bus service connecting with an Underground station. The benefits of London itself highlighted by the posters were also mainly those to be enjoyed at leisure – museums, theatres, cinemas, shops, parks, sporting events, or simply the sights of London.

Writing in 1927 after nearly twenty years' experience in commissioning posters, Pick commented on the purpose which they had been intended to fulfil: 'It may be supposed that their purpose is immediately directed to securing passengers. In some instances this has been the case, but in as many instances the purpose has been the establishment of goodwill and good understanding between the passengers and the companies. A transport service is continually open to criticism and much of the criticism arises from a lack of knowledge. Every passenger is a potential critic; many passengers are dynamic ones. So there has been an attempt to place before the public all the pertinent facts underlying the success of the Underground in an attractive and readily comprehendable form. Even when the purpose has been to secure passengers it has been the practice to proceed by indirect means. To create a feeling of restlessness, a distaste for the immediate surroundings, to revive that desire for change, which all inherit from their barbarian ancestors . . .' It was typical of Pick to express the functional practicalities of running a transport business with a tinge of romance.

In an age before market research it would have been difficult to quantify the impact of the posters with any precision, and the Underground rarely attempted to do so. In 1922 the staff magazine announced that while in 1913 the companies had spent £32,000 on advertising and carried 1,124 million passengers, in 1921 they spent £60,000 and carried 1,461 million. 'In advertising the Underground, London itself is advertised. Millions of people through the year now look to the Underground announcements to decide how they shall travel and what place of amusement or country excursion they should choose. Londoners know their way about better and enjoy their London far more since the Underground began to address them by posters.'

THE UNDERGROUND AS ART PATRON

This increased expenditure on advertising largely reflected the rising output of posters, although by the early 1920s the Underground was also using other media to promote itself, such as guidebooks and almost daily press advertisements. As the poster programme grew, Pick experimented continually with new artists and different approaches. Finding insufficient

By 1913, the free maps issued by the London General Omnibus Company were carrying a simplified version of their earlier device. Shorn of its wings and wheel spokes, it was essentially an early form of the bar and circle.

range and quality in the commercial artists used by the printers, he soon began arranging direct commissions himself, encouraging fine artists as well as illustrators to try their hand at poster design. This in turn gave the Underground a growing reputation as a patron, and artists began taking their work to Pick in the hope of getting a commission. He would consider unknown and established artists alike, often trying out young artists recommended to him through the art schools, although never compromising on standards.

An artist when commissioned would usually be given a fairly broad brief. A title and subject for the illustration would be suggested, but initially the lettering was usually the responsibility of the printers and not the artist. By the 1920s, however, the typographical input was being determined by the Underground's own design staff, and generally involved setting the poster text in Johnston. Artists were allowed considerable scope for self-expression in the pictorial content, although the final artwork was as likely to remain unused

A tube car interior in 1932 during overhaul at Acton Works, with most of the internal advertising removed. On the right, a poster by Tom Purvis (reproduced on page 73) demonstrates the use of the glass draught screens for the display of small panel posters produced to advertise special events such as major exhibitions.

A poster display at St James's Park station in 1935, carefully delineated by a grid of decorative borders. As the London Transport Head Office at 55 Broadway was directly above this station, standards would have been particularly high here, but the strict grid layout was used throughout the system. The upper posters are by the prolific Walter Spradbery, whose work is well represented in this book. Those at the left and right below are by Adrian Allinson.

as printed. Edward Bawden recalls that his first work for the Underground, commissioned on the recommendation of his tutor at the Royal College of Art who knew Pick, nearly came to grief. It was to be an illustrated map poster of the 1924 British Empire Exhibition at Wembley. Pick rejected his first proposal and brought in a more experienced designer, Thomas Derrick, to handle the cartography. Bawden was left to provide the illustrations to Derrick's overall map design.

Pick's method was to buy almost twice as many designs as the Underground would eventually use. There were no fixed fees. The company paid bigger fees to its more established artists, thereby setting extremely high standards while encouraging a very broad range of approaches, and getting the best possible choice. Pick never imposed his own taste, but judged the works on their 'fitness for purpose', their effectiveness as posters. 'There is room in posters for all styles,' he once commented. 'They are the most eclectic form of art. It is possible to move from the most literal representation to the wildest impressionism as long as the subject remains understandable to the man in the street.'

As Pick rose through the Underground organization and his responsibilities increased, he was able to apply h s high design standards to other aspects of the company. His publicity role, originally described as Traffic Officer, was expanded to that of Commercial Officer in 1912. By 1921 he was Joint Assistant Managing Director and from 1928 Joint Managing Director. Finally, in 1933, when the Underground Group became part of the new London Passenger Transport Board, he became Ashfield's immediate deputy, as Vice Chairman and Chief Executive.

Under Pick's influence good design became the hallmark of the Underground and of London Transport. He brought in the architect Charles Holden to design new stations and other buildings in the mid-1920s, creating a distinctive new house style. Holden's work is now recognized as being among the best commercial architecture in Britain between the wars, a discreet blend of traditional and modern materials and forms. New buses and Underground trains set increasingly high standards of functional elegance and efficient engineering that were internationally admired. Pick insisted on quality and careful attention to detail in every item of equipment, right down to the design of the seat upholstery, light fittings and litter bins. Everything, however small, contributed to the overall effect and he believed that London's bus and Underground services should be seen as modern, efficient, self-respecting and confident.

His impact was that of a benevolent design dictator. The Underground and London Transport gave him, in Nikolaus Pevsner's words, 'a free hand to combine large-scale organization and administration with large-scale propaganda for the visual expression of honesty, harmony and order. He thought in terms of visual propaganda in whatever he did. His new buildings, his rolling stock, his innumerable pieces of excellent industrial design, helped to make streets better and ultimately towns better.' But of all his design interests, Pick kept the closest watch on the posters, the area where his management had begun. Even as Chief Executive of London Transport he would still insist on vetting poster designs, although direct responsibility for commissioning them was eventually delegated to a Publicity Officer, Christian Barman, who was appointed in 1935.

ART FOR ALL

During the 1920s and 1930s the Underground's posters became more than a medium for promoting the transport services. They effectively turned every Underground station and bus shelter into a venue for constantly changing exhibitions of modern art. Many of the artists commissioned by the Underground were influenced by the avant-garde European art movements of the early twentieth century, and posters became a medium for popular commercial interpretation of these styles. Cubism, Futurism and Vorticism all reached the general public in Britain by way of the Underground poster. The simplification of images into dramatic, geometrically based compositions – which was common to all these new art movements – was ,particularly appropriate to poster design, and stimulated an exciting new creative approach by commercial artists. Edward McKnight Kauffer, the American designer first commissioned by Pick in 1915, was the most influential of the 'new wave' of commercial artists. He claimed to be applying scientific principles in his use of modern artistic expression in advertising: 'Non-representative and geometrical pattern designs can in effect strike a sledge-hammer blow if handled by a sensitive designer possessing a knowledge of the action of colour on the average man or woman,' he wrote in 1921.

Whether the Underground genuinely influenced popular artistic taste through its posters is debatable, but there were numerous claims for it at the time. The art critic Anthony Blunt, writing on Kauffer's work in 1935, suggested that 'apart from producing admirable posters, McKnight Kauffer has rendered another important service to modern art. By using the methods of the more advanced schools, and by putting them before the men in the street in such a way as to catch them off their guard, so that they are lured into liking the poster before they realise that it is just the kind of thing

which they loathe in the exhibition gallery, by this means he has familiarized a very wide public with the conventions of modern painting and has greatly increased the chances which modern painters, who are not involved with publicity, have of being appreciated and widely enjoyed.'

Blunt's claim, however, was certainly not supported by the sales figures. A typical print-run in the 1920s was 1,000, of which 850 were required for posting on the system where they were displayed for one month. The remaining 150 copies were available for purchase at the company's head office for between two and five shillings, depending on the printing cost. Posters in demand with the public were invariably those which followed the more traditional artistic styles, such as Gregory Brown's *St Albans* (page 37), Fred Taylor's *Kew* (page 39) and Dorothy Burroughes' *For the Zoo* (page 66). These three were all in the top ten of a bestsellers' list which was announced by the Underground in 1923.

Of course, there were those for whom even Gregory Brown's landscapes in bright, flat colour appeared dis-

The poster store at Charing Cross in 1943, with its wartime staff of women workers. The poster on the table is reproduced on page 105.

concertingly modern. This Cockney lament entitled *A Plaint to the Poster Artist* by M. E. Durham appeared in *The Manchester Guardian* in the 1920s:

Oh, I want to see the country
Like when I was a boy –
When the sky was blue and the clouds was white
And the green fields was a joy

I want to see the country
But the posters seem to show
The country ain't no more the place
Like what I used to know

For the sky is pink and the fields are mauve
And the cottages all turned yellow
And the sheep all green or tangerine
Enough to stun a fellow

Oh, I want to see the country
And I wouldn't mind where I went ter
So long as I knoo the trees weren't blue
And the cows all turned magenter!

Even the serious-minded Pick evidently found this amusing: it was recently discovered, carefully retyped, among his surviving private papers.

It seems that only the discerning few bought works by Kauffer and his fellow Modernists. Sebastian Flyte, narrator of Evelyn Waugh's novel *Brideshead Revisited*, decorates his college room at Oxford in the 1920s with a Kauffer, presumably a reflection of Waugh's own youthful taste. Edward Bawden has also recalled that he and Eric Ravilious, when students together at the Royal College of Art in the 1920s, looked foward eagerly to the appearance of a new Kauffer Underground poster which was then, literally, one of the cheapest forms of good modern art available, less than half the price of comparable reproductions sold by organizations such as the Modern Art Society.

Whatever the posters' reception by the passengers, the response of the press was nearly always favourable. Where once the Underground company had been sniped at as an American-based interloper bringing alien ways to London, by the 1920s it had become a respected part of the corporate establishment. The company's patronage of good art and design probably achieved much more in improved public relations than it did as a form of direct advertising.

There were discordant notes. Roger Fry was one of the few leading art critics to introduce a touch of cynicism about the way the Underground and its imitators were using posters in the 1920s. 'Advertisement has, in recent times, taken on a new complexion,' he wrote in 1926. 'It is tinged with a new poetry – a new romance. It is no longer the

severely practical affair it once was; it brings about a new relation between the public and the great limited liability companies. There is a note of affectionate zeal for the public in their communications. The big companies pose as the friends and advisors of the public, they appear filled with concern for their welfare, they would even educate them and show them the way to higher and better things. The Underground tells the slum dweller of the beauties of nature in the country, it reveals the wonders of animal life at the Zoo, it inspires the historical sense by pictures of old London.

At the height of its publicity drive in the 1920s, the Underground was promoting itself almost daily in the newspapers with paid advertising. Many of these press advertisements were text only, but some featured illustrations by artists who were also commissioned for poster work. This example is from a set of leisure advertisements illustrated by Edward Bawden in 1928.

'The great railway combines tell us of the glories of provincial England, and inspire an enthusiasm for the grandeur of modern locomotives. In fact, each of these great concerns tries to build up in the public imagination an image of something almost personal – and as such they begin to claim almost the loyalty and allegiance of the public they exploit. They produce in the public a non-critical state of romantic enthusiasm for the line. More and more the whole thing takes on an air of romance and unreality.

'In all this matter of hypnotism on a large scale the poster has become the great weapon of the industrial companies, and the poster designer their great ally.'

But Fry's was very much a minority view and, as he himself recognized, the new approach to poster advertising spearheaded by the Underground was extremely influential. The main-line railway companies, whose early poster designs were generally rather conservative exercises in pictorialism, began to emulate the Underground with more experimental work, though never on the same scale. Government bodies such as the General Post Office and the Empire Marketing Board took up similar poster campaigns, the latter using Pick as their advisor in commissioning posters to encourage consumers to buy products from the British Empire. Commercial organizations such as the Shell oil company also adopted the art poster, reproducing the work of specially commissioned artists on large billboards on the sides of their lorries. For some years, certainly until the end of the 1930s, it was the Underground and London Transport that set the national pace in poster advertising; others followed.

PICK'S LEGACY

Frank Pick left London Transport in 1940, served briefly as Director General of the wartime Ministry of Information, and died in 1941. Nikolaus Pevsner, writing in *The Architectural Review* a year after his death, described him as 'the greatest patron of the arts whom this century has so far produced in England, and indeed the ideal patron of the age.' He was irreplaceable at London Transport, but fortunately the poster tradition that he had established was not lost. After the inevitable economies and cutbacks of wartime, a new Publicity Officer, Harold F. Hutchison, was appointed in 1947. He had been copy chief and creative designer with some major UK advertising agencies, notably Vernon's and Linton's. Hutchison accepted the post on his own terms, which specifically included overall control of the poster programme, on which he reported solely to the Chairman.

While recognizing the value of maintaining the Pick tradition, Hutchison was also aware of the changing circumstances of London Transport's operations, which made it necessary to adapt the publicity message in the posters. With more people using the services than ever before, there was no need to encourage travel. 'Today our Traffic Department would actually be happier if people travelled less, especially during peak hours,' he wrote in a staff magazine article in 1947, explaining his policy. 'The present function of our poster publicity, therefore, is different. It is to be London Transport's information window through which we tell the public what we do and what we hope to do; what we expect of our staff and what we appreciate from our public . . . . instead of the competitive simplicity of "Go By Underground" we have the more difficult but more interesting theme of explaining the largest urban passenger transport system in the world to those who must use it.'

By about 1918, the solid red disc had become a circle: the exact proportions were devised by Edward Johnston to suit his newly designed lettering. The symbol was registered as a copyright design, and was used throughout the 1920s on signs, posters and other publicity material. In 1972, the proportions were slightly changed to produce the symbol we know today.

In practice, this change of direction did not produce a recognizable change in the balance of the pictorial poster publicity. The best of the newly commissioned posters continued to advise travellers of off-peak leisure travel destinations in London's countryside or of the attractions of the central area. Those which explained how London Transport worked were, with a few exceptions, more mundane productions which had little creative sparkle.

One of Hutchison's innovations was the pair poster arrangement. For prime sites, such as the entrances to Underground stations, the main publicity posters were designed in two halves, each the size of a standard 40 × 25 in double royal. One was entirely pictorial, while the other half was given a border design by the same artist to act as a matching frame, but was largely given over to text. This gave both the artist/designer and the copywriter more space and freedom to develop an idea, although by encouraging the use

A typical example of Charles Holden's functional Underground station architecture of the 1930s, combining lighting column, station name and poster display boards in one unit. This picture, taken in 1950, shows one of the new pair posters introduced after the war. The subject is *Country Church* by Denys Nichols, featuring the artist's work uncluttered by text on the left and a text panel on the right framed by a matching decorative border design.

15

of more text it also somewhat diminished the overall impact and immediacy of the poster design.

INTO THE PRESENT DAY

The number of pictorial posters issued by London Transport after the war never returned to pre-war levels. In the 1920s the Underground was regularly producing over forty a year; by the 1950s this was down to seven or eight. The use of pictorial posters was no longer considered a prime medium of publicity, and there were increasing pressures to cut the budget allocation for commissioning artists. At the same time fewer young artists and designers seemed interested: poster work no longer offered the same challenges. As it gradually ceased to be seen as the favoured medium for avant-garde design, so it no longer attracted the range of innovation and talent of the inter-war years. London Transport was no longer actively trying to encourage new talent, but tended to play safer in its commissions.

Hutchison retired in the mid-1960s and was succeeded by his long-time deputy Bryce Beaumont, who had written copy for London Transport posters since before the war. Beaumont maintained the pictorial poster programme, but at a progressively reduced level. At a time when London Transport faced mounting problems – staff shortages, spiralling costs and falling passenger numbers – the traditional soft sell of its elegant publicity posters no longer seemed appropriate to the organization's needs. There was a growing view that posters of this kind were an anachronism and that London Transport's advertising and publicity should be geared more closely to achieving direct and measurable results.

In the 1970s a central marketing department was established and an increasing amount of London Transport's advertising work was contracted out to the agency FCB – Foote, Cone and Belding. By 1975, when Michael Levey took over from Beaumont as Publicity Officer, the number of posters directly commissioned from artists and designers in the old way had fallen to about four a year. Even this limited programme effectively ceased by the end of the decade, after which nearly all advertising work was conducted through the agency. Posters formed only a minor part of the new marketing strategy, which for the first time included radio and television advertising. There were occasional flashes of inspiration, but the advertising posters were mostly photographic, and few compared well with the best in commercial graphic design.

'ART ON THE UNDERGROUND'

Then, in the mid-1980s, a new marketing initiative brought art back to the Underground poster in a rather different form. London Underground's Marketing and Development Director, Dr Henry Fitzhugh, took the decision in 1986 to revive the policy of direct commissions to artists. The resulting poster programme differed from previous campaigns in that it was not intended either as advertising or as publicity. 'Art on the Underground' was to be a scheme for displaying newly commissioned fine art in poster form, and was planned and funded quite separately from the Underground's main advertising and publicity campaigns. It was essentially conceived as a means of corporate art sponsorship, whereby London Underground would commission original works of art and reproduce them as posters. The subjects would be loosely connected with the Underground as possible destinations, but generating travel was not their prime purpose. Advertising and publicity posters would continue to be produced by an agency, at that time still FCB Advertising.

At its most basic level, the new art poster programme was a way of filling blank, unsold advertising space on the Underground with images which improved the general appearance of the passenger environment. The cost of this approach was no more than would be required to create advertising 'fillers' from any other source. But Fitzhugh was adamant that he was not simply using posters as decorative wallpaper for tube stations. His stated intention was to use the programme 'to promote art, especially fine art, and its appreciation among our customers, and to promote young artists'.

The Underground became a patron of the arts again, at least on a limited scale. Fitzhugh re-established a policy of direct commissioning from both new and established artists. Many well-known painters responded with enthusiasm to the suggestion that they provide, for a modest fee, works of art that would enhance the public environment. He began by opting for a mix of the safe and the more daring. Each year he commissioned two 'easy' subjects, two more avant-garde works, and two that fell roughly in the middle. 'I don't want to get so far ahead of the public that we lose it,' he explained. These six posters a year were printed in editions of 6,000 each, and remained posted in the Underground for several months to a year. They might then be reprinted in a smaller size for further use. If a poster proved especially popular, the print run could be repeated. This happened with David Booth's Tate Gallery (page 128) and Jennie Tuffs' New Kew (page 133), which both sold in their thousands to the public. Fitzhugh's aim was 'to strike a balance, so that fine art which is popular with our customers continues to make a major impact on the visual appeal of the Underground. The passengers, the artists and the Underground will be all the better for it'.

Fitzhugh left London Underground in the early 1990s, and the art programme was reviewed in a tighter economic climate. 'Art on the Underground' was no longer needed to fill unsold poster space on stations. London Transport Advertising, which managed the commercial poster sites on the Underground and buses, was privatized and TDI, its new owners, started selling poster space more aggressively. However, a market research study showed that the art poster programme was popular with the Underground's customers, who liked to be presented with attractive images that were not offering a 'hard sell' provided that the message could be understood by all. It was a conclusion that Frank Pick had reached, rather more intuitively, over sixty years earlier, but it provided the business case for continuing with the art programme, though linked more obviously with specifically targeted marketing campaigns.

London Transport's Director of Design, Jeremy Rewse Davies, took over the programme of commissioning new artworks, though with a reduced budget. New art posters now appeared for the first time since the 1970s on dedicated advertising space, reflecting the increased involvement of the Advertising and Publicity Department and a new working agreement on posting arrangements with TDI, whose logo appeared on the posters. A new Director of Marketing, Geoff Ellerton, was appointed and in due course he and Charlie Edelman, who had become Head of Advertising and Publicity, further refined the art programme to include use of the artworks on leaflets and distribution displays as well as the standard poster format.

The London Transport Museum, as the principal sales outlet for new posters as well as being the home of the historic poster archive, also became more closely involved in the process of commissioning new artworks. At the same time the quality and inventiveness of the posters commissioned by the Advertising and Publicity Department improved dramatically as campaigns were opened up to competitive pitches from different advertising agencies. Some imaginative recent examples created by Bainsfair Sharkey Trott and BMP [Bose Massimi Pollitt] are reproduced here (pages 142, 144–7 and 150–1).

In some respects the use of posters by London's transport services has come full circle. Attempting to draw a clear distinction between 'fine art' commissions which are turned into posters and the commercial work produced by graphic designers is as pointless now as it was in the 1920s. Suffice it to say that fine art still does not always translate well into poster reproduction and a graphic designer working to a commercial brief will often produce a far more creative and effective poster. The old debate about whether an original work of art created in oils on canvas is inherently superior to one designed using photography or computer generated images and then mass reproduced is also both redundant and irrelevant. The most encouraging final thought is that nearly a hundred years after the London Underground issued its first pictorial posters, the medium is still being put to thoughtful and creative use, brightening the daily travelling environment for millions of people in the biggest art gallery in the world. Long may it continue.

THE POSTERS

PRINTING AND PRODUCTION

All the posters reproduced in this book were originally printed by lithography. This is a chemical process which relies on the simple fact that grease and water do not mix. The artist's design, which may be in any medium, is first transferred on to the printing surface. Originally this would have been a block of limestone, but since the turn of the century metal printing plates have been used for most commercial lithography. Areas to be printed are treated with a greasy medium to accept ink and reject water. The background is then treated to accept water and repel ink. This ensures that only the image area retains ink and prints on to the paper when the stone or plate is run through the printing press. The key colours of the poster are built up by overprinting each one separately.

Today, the artist's design is transferred to the printing plates photographically, but in the early years of the century it had to be literally re-drawn for reproduction. The craftsmen who carried out this work for commercial printers performed a vital role in poster production, which could often involve making subtle changes to the artist's design in order to make the best use of the printing process. Skilled lithographers were not merely copyists but artistic interpreters whose creative contribution to the final poster design was rarely acknowledged.

The early posters were printed either on flat bed lithographic machines made originally for printing from lithographic stones and converted to take metal plates, or on direct rotary machines using zinc plates held in position round a cylinder. In about 1910 the first 'offset' rotary machines were introduced. Here an intermediate cylinder covered with a rubber blanket is introduced between the printing plate and the paper. The inked image is transferred first to the rubber blanket then on to the paper, reducing the risk of damage to the delicate metal plate. In the days of hand-drawn lithography it also simplified the process of transferring the original design on to the printing plates because it was no longer necessary to reverse the image. Offset litho rotary machines became the standard method of commercial poster printing and this remains the case today despite the introduction and use of digital images and printing in recent years.

SIZES AND DATES

The standard poster size used by the Underground for over eighty years is the 40 x 25 in. 'double royal', a format used almost exclusively by railway companies. Most of the posters in this book were printed to these dimensions.

Smaller 30 x 20 in. 'double crown' posters were originally produced for display on the front panels of buses and the side panels of trams. For the recent 'Art on the Underground' campaign the 60 x 40 in. four-sheet size was used, together with double crown versions grouped in blocks of four to fit the same area.

The small panel posters produced in the 1920s and '30s for Underground car interiors vary in size because they were not designed to fit a standard frame or wall space but were displayed on the glass draught screens just inside the doors.

Throughout this book, the dates given in the captions are printing dates.

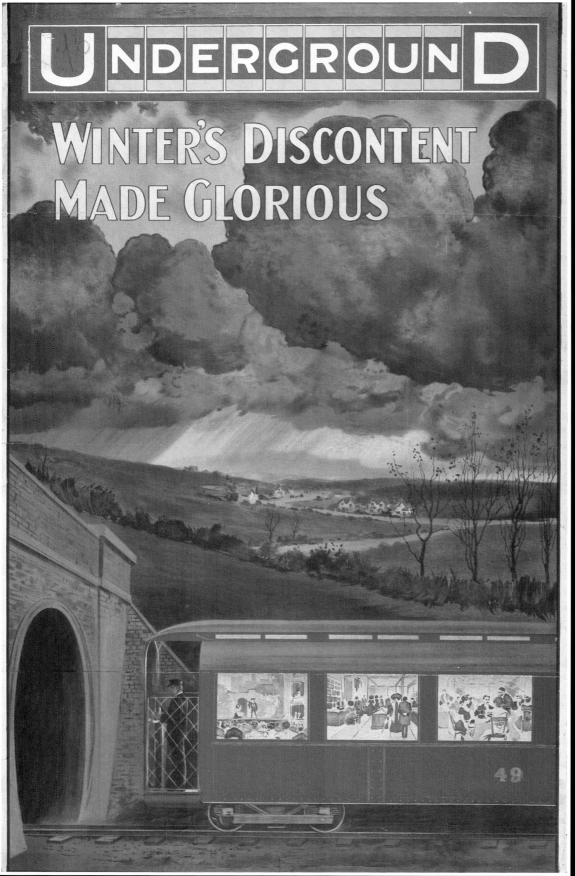

UNDERGROUND

WINTER'S DISCONTENT MADE GLORIOUS

49

WINTER'S DISCONTENT MADE
GLORIOUS
ARTIST UNKNOWN
1909
40 × 25 in/101.6 × 63.5 cm

THE UNDERGROUND was often
promoted in early posters as a
refuge from the English climate.
Copywriters borrowed
liberally from the literature of
the past, in this case adapting
Shakespeare to create the
slogan.

MANY LONDONERS became regular travellers for the first time in the Edwardian period. Daily journeys to work by electric tube train and motor-bus trips to the country on Sundays were novelties in the early 1900s but commonplace by 1914. The Underground Group's colourful poster publicity, introduced from 1908

onwards, gave its constituent companies a substantial advantage over their competitors and helped establish the Group as the major transport operator in the capital. The standard of poster design was extremely high from the start, with a series of eye-catching designs and the first move towards a coherent graphic identity in the use of block lettering.

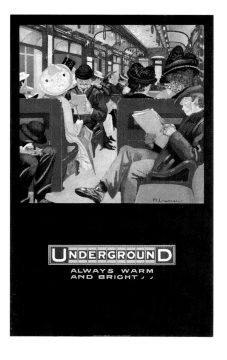

ALWAYS WARM AND BRIGHT
MARC LAURENCE
1912
40 × 25 in/101.6 × 63.5 cm

THIS UNDERGROUND car interior is represented in the bright, exaggerated colours favoured by Matisse and the Fauves.

WHEN IN DOUBT
JOHN HASSALL
1913
40 × 25 in/101.6 × 63.5 cm

HULLO! DID YOU COME BY
UNDERGROUND?
MABEL LUCIE ATTWELL
1913
40 × 25 in/101.6 × 63.5 cm

THE DISTRICT RAILWAY built up a substantial off-peak traffic running organized day-trips for Sunday Schools and children's clubs to what was then the countryside just beyond London. The Pavilion pleasure grounds at Eastcote, run by Captain Albert Bailey of the Salvation Army, was a particularly popular destination. Mabel Lucie Attwell's chubby toddlers were already familiar from thousands of her picture postcards issued by Valentine's of Dundee in the two years before this poster appeared.

NO NEED TO ASK A P'LICEMAN!
JOHN HASSALL
1908
20¼ × 23 in/51.4 × 58.4 cm

JOHN HASSALL was among the few well established names in commercial art at the turn of the century, and an obvious choice for one of the Underground's first pictorial posters. After designing a number of successful theatre posters, he had moved into advertising work and produced a series of humorous designs for Colman's Mustard, Nestlé, Veritas Gas Mantles and the British Vacuum Cleaner Company. His Underground posters are in much the same comic style. Hassall's best-known poster, which appeared shortly after 'No need to ask a P'liceman!', was for the Great Northern Railway and shows a jolly fisherman running along a beach above the memorable slogan, 'Skegness is So Bracing!'

"FLEET upon fleet ; argosy upon argosy. Masts to the right, masts to the left, masts in front, masts yonder above the warehouses ; masts in among the streets as steeples appear amid roofs ; masts across the river hung with drooping half-furled sails ; masts afar down thin and attenuated, mere dark straight lines in the distance. They await in stillness the rising of the tide." Richard Jefferies in "Nature near London."

UNDERGROUND

THE WAY OF BUSINESS

LONDON DOCKS AT WAPPING OR ROTHERHITHE STATIONS

THE WESTMINSTER PRESS

THE WAY OF BUSINESS
FRANK BRANGWYN
1913
40 × 25 in/101.6 × 63.5 cm

FOR BUSINESS OR PLEASURE
F. C. WITNEY
1913
25 × 40 in/63.5 × 101.6 cm

THE WAY FOR ALL
ALFRED FRANCE
1911
40 × 25 in/101.6 × 63.5 cm

EARLY Underground advertising was not targeted at particular social groups but was deliberately designed to have a universal appeal, summed up in the 'Way for All' slogan used here. Tube travel was classless, although a distinction between first and third class was retained on the District Railway. This meant that, unlike the main line railways, the Underground could offer the lure of comfortable travel on equal terms to rich and poor alike. The passengers shown in F. C. Witney's 1913 poster are a reasonable mix of social types, although it is noticeable that the more obviously wealthy and fashionable are shown in the foreground. Brangwyn's London Docks scene depicts only the labouring classes, but there is no suggestion that they have travelled to work by Underground. The Docks are presented simply as one of the spectacles of the city, to be visited and marvelled at.

PADDINGTON NEW STATION
CHARLES SHARLAND
1913
40 × 25 in/101.6 × 63.5 cm

LIGHT, POWER AND SPEED
CHARLES SHARLAND
1910
40 × 25 in/101.6 × 63.5 cm

THESE TWO POSTERS emphasize the modernity of the Underground all of it reliant on electrical power, which totally transformed urban life in the Edwardian period. 'Light, Power and Speed' features one of the new trains introduced with the electrification of the District Railway in 1905. Escalators, then called 'moving staircases', were first introduced at Earl's Court station in 1911 between the District and Piccadilly line platforms. The new Bakerloo tube station at Paddington, which opened two years later, was one of the first to be designed with escalators instead of lifts.

GOLDERS GREEN
ARTIST UNKNOWN
1908
40 × 25 in/101.6 × 63.5 cm

'GOLDERS GREEN' was the first of many posters encouraging house-hunters to move out to the newly developed areas on the rural fringes of London which were being opened up by the Underground. Golders Green in North London was the first Edwardian Underground suburb. Before the arrival of the Hampstead tube in 1907 it was little more than a country crossroads. Within a few months the new terminus was the focus of a new community, complete with shops and avenues of Arts and Crafts style houses. Just to the north the first section of Henrietta Barnett's model housing development, Hampstead Garden Suburb, was laid out over the next few years.

FLYING AT HENDON
TONY SARG
1913
40 × 25 in/101.6 × 63.5 cm

THE OPEN ROAD
WALTER SPRADBERY
1914
40 × 25 in/101.6 × 63.5 cm

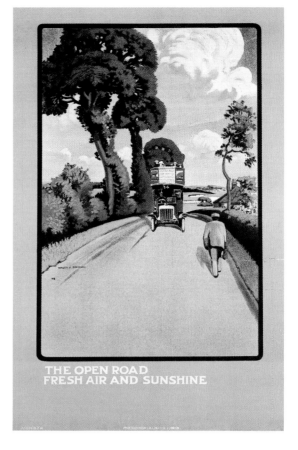

THE HOMEWARD WAY
WALTER SPRADBERY
1914
40 × 25 in/101.6 × 63.5 cm

KEW
S. T. C. WEEKS
1913
40 × 25 in/101.6 × 63.5 cm

BOAT RACE
CHARLES SHARLAND
1913
40 × 25 in/101.6 × 63.5 cm

POSTER ADVERTISING was soon
extended to the Underground Group's
subsidiary bus and tram companies.
The capital's main bus operator, the
London General Omnibus Company,
became part of the Underground
Group in 1913 – this was just two
years after it had replaced its last horse
bus. With a fully mechanized fleet it
was possible to operate over much
longer routes, and a number of
services running out into London's
countryside were introduced. Nearly
all the early road services posters
promoted leisure travel by these
country routes, or trips to special
events like the annual University Boat
Race on the Thames or flying days at
Hendon aerodrome.

750 · Nº 479 · II · 13

WATERLOW & SONS LTD LITH LONDON WALL LONDON

JAPAN-BRITISH EXHIBITION
ARTIST UNKNOWN
1910
40 × 25 in/101.6 × 63.5 cm

THE POPULAR SERVICE SUITS ALL TASTES
ARTIST UNKNOWN
1913
40 × 25 in/101.6 × 63.5 cm

UNDERGROUND POSTERS offered an opportunity for artists to experiment, and a wide variety of stylistic influences from both the fine and decorative arts was apparent. Here they include an anonymous pastiche of the Willow Pattern china decoration!

FOR THE SUNDAY CONCERTS
FRED TAYLOR
1912
40 × 25 in/101.6 × 63.5 cm

WAR
TO ARMS CITIZENS OF THE EMPIRE!!

WAR – TO ARMS CITIZENS OF THE EMPIRE!!
FRANK BRANGWYN
1915
40 × 25 in/101.6 × 63.5 cm

THE UNDERGROUND'S poster publicity served a wider social purpose during the First World War, including this call to recruitment published before the introduction of conscription in 1916.

2

DURING THE FIRST WORLD WAR the Underground Group's posters took on a propaganda function in addition to their publicity role. This created some rather curious mixed messages in the early part of the war. Travel posters still promoted pleasure trips on the system as if nothing had changed, but were often

1914-18

displayed alongside sombre army recruiting posters also issued by the Underground. As the war dragged on it was clearly not appropriate to continue encouraging leisure travel, but the romantic appeal of London's countryside was used in posters sent out by the Underground to the troops overseas as 'reminders of home.'

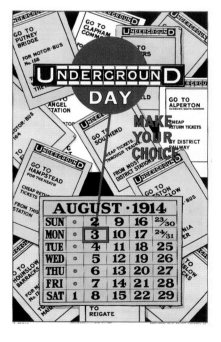

UNDERGROUND DAY – MAKE YOUR CHOICE
ARTIST UNKNOWN
1914
40 × 25 in/101.6 × 63.5 cm

WHILE LONDONERS made their choice of Underground excursion for the August Bank Holiday of 1914, politicians were making more serious decisions about the future of Europe. By the end of the week Britain was at war with Germany.

THE ONLY ROAD FOR AN ENGLISHMAN
GERALD SPENCER PRYSE
1914
40 × 25 in/101.6 × 63.5 cm

INVADE IT YOURSELF
WARBIS BROTHERS
1915
40 × 25 in/101.6 × 63.5 cm

THESE TWO POSTERS show a surprising contrast in the treatment of war. Spencer Pryse's sombre, low-key propaganda poster was published by the Underground shortly before the Warbis Brothers' jaunty appeal to forget about the conflict and carry on as normal. The drawing for 'The Only Road' was actually made at the Front, straight on to lithographic stones which the artist carried around in his car.

WHY BOTHER ABOUT THE GERMANS INVADING THE COUNTRY?

INVADE IT YOURSELF
BY UNDERGROUND AND MOTOR-'BUS

EASTER · 1915

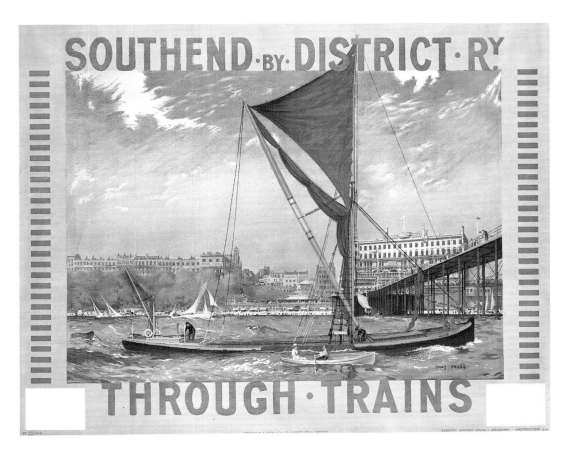

SOUTHEND
CHARLES PEARS
1915
25 × 40 in/63.5 × 101.6 cm

MOST Underground posters ignored the war completely and continued to encourage leisure travel. Southend was the only seaside resort advertised on the Underground because a through service was available from the District Railway. Special trains ran from Ealing Broadway, hauled by electric locomotives on the Underground as far as Barking where a London, Tilbury & Southend Railway steam locomotive took over for the run to the coast.

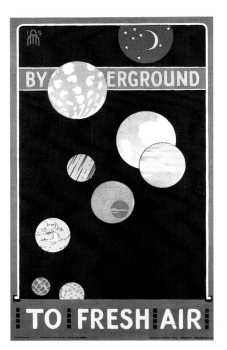

TO FRESH AIR
MAXWELL ARMFIELD
1915
40 × 25 in/101.6 × 63.5 cm

TAKE
YOUR FAMILY
TO

BANK HOLIDAY
AUGUST 2ND 1915

TAKE YOUR FAMILY
AGNES RICHARDSON
1915
40 × 25 in/101.6 × 63.5 cm

HAMPSTEAD HEATH
NANCY SMITH
1915
40 × 25 in/101.6 × 63.5 cm

HAMPSTEAD HEATH

THE NEAREST POINT TO LONDON
FOR FUN AND FRESH AIR

BY
UNDERGROUND

THE NORTH DOWNS
E. McKnight Kauffer
1916
30 × 20 in/76.2 × 50.8 cm

REIGATE
E. McKnight Kauffer
1916
30 × 20 in/76.2 × 50.8 cm

St Albans
F. Gregory Brown
1916
30 × 20 in/76.2 × 50.8 cm

AMONG THE NEW TALENT discovered
by Frank Pick during the war years
were Edward McKnight Kauffer and
Gregory Brown, both to become
renowned as poster artists in the
1920s. Although their styles later
diverged considerably, their early
posters show a remarkable similarity of
approach. Kauffer was a young
American artist living in Paris who
moved to England at the outbreak of
war. He took his work to show Pick on
the advice of John Hassall, and the
resulting commission marked the
beginning of a professional relationship
that was to last for 25 years. The
Underground became Kauffer's main
client, for whom he eventually
designed over a hundred posters, and
he in turn became their major artist.
Brown, three years older than Kauffer,
began his working life apprenticed to
an art metalworker, but abandoned
this to become an illustrator. While
Kauffer was later to experiment
continually with new ideas and became
a leading advocate of Modernist
graphic design in Britain, Brown was
soon one of the major exponents of
the brightly coloured rural landscape,
as shown here, always using vivid and
well-defined tones that were easily
translated into a lithographic poster.

The Underground Railways of London, knowing how many of their passengers are now engaged on important business in France and other parts of the world, send out this reminder of home. Thanks are due to George Clausen R.A. for the drawing.

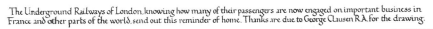

A WISH } Mine be a cot beside the hill; | The swallow, oft beneath my thatch | Around my ivied porch shall spring | ¶The village church among the trees.
A bee-hive's hum shall soothe my ear; | Shall twitter from her clay-built nest: | Each fragrant flower that drinks the dew, | Where first our marriage vows were given,
A willowy brook that turns a mill, | Oft shall the pilgrim lift the latch, | And Lucy, at her wheel, shall sing | With merry peals shall swell the breeze
With many a fall shall linger near; | And share my meal, a welcome guest: | In russet gown and apron blue. | And point with taper spire to Heaven. SAMUEL ROGERS

A WISH
GEORGE CLAUSEN
1917
40 × 25 in/101.6 × 63.5 cm

HARVEST
J. WALTER WEST
1916
40 × 60 n/101.6 × 152.4 cm

SOME OF THE POSTERS published by the
Underground during the war were not
primarily intended for sites on the
system, but were sent to troops
overseas to decorate army billets and.
as the official description put it, to
'awaken thoughts of pleasant homely
things'. The only visual reference to the
war in these scenes is the fact that the
harvesting is being carried out entirely
by women.

LONDON MEMORIES, KEW GARDENS
FRED TAYLOR
1918
30 × 20 in/76.2 × 50.8 cm

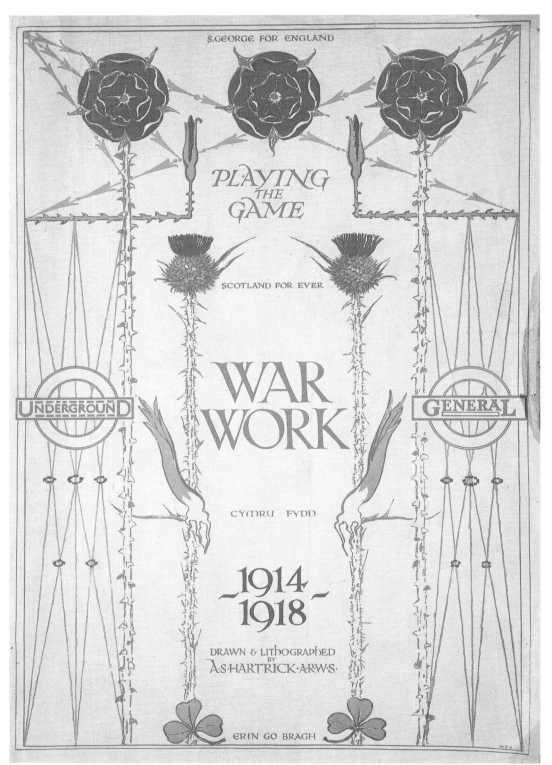

PLAYING THE GAME – WAR WORK
A. S. HARTRICK
1919
20 × 12 in/50.8 × 30.5 cm (each print)

FOUR EXAMPLES, and the cover, from a set of commemorative lithographs published by the Underground to show the contribution to war work made by its staff. As men left to join the forces, women were recruited to replace them in many jobs such as the bus conductor and Underground lift attendant shown here. Each of these portraits has a border relating it to the war. Below the bus driver are London buses on active service carrying troops to the Western Front. The signalman at Earl's Court is framed by searchlights picking out a Zeppelin airship on a bombing raid over London. The lift scene is linked to the battle front by the Dover Street sign: trenches were often given street names from home by the troops. In this case, t also refers to a tube station: Dover Street, on the Piccadilly Line, was re-named Green Park in 1933.

WHERE IT IS
WARM AND BRIGHT

UNDERGROUND

1366. 1000. 2C-8-24.   VINCENT BROOKS DAY & SON Ltd. Lith. London.W.C.2.

WHERE IT IS WARM AND BRIGHT
V. L. DANVERS
1924
40 × 25 in/101.6 × 63.5 cm

A PERFECT EXAMPLE of 'soft sell' advertising from the heyday of the Underground poster, this evocative image of the city draws the eye to the Underground symbol, which beckons like a familiar beacon in the gloom.

3 THE 1920S AND EARLY 1930S were the heyday of the Underground poster, both in quality and quantity. It was a period of rapid growth for the system, with the provision of new and improved road and rail services including some major extensions. Under Frank Pick's management the company established a clear corporate

1918-33

design identity in everything from architecture to publicity. An adventurous commissioning policy at a time when artists were experimenting with new graphic styles produced an astonishing range of posters to which the Johnston typeface gave a strong visual coherence. The Underground Group became an important patron of the arts and the acknowledged leader in the field of poster publicity.

TAKE YOUR PARTY BY SALOON
COACH
VICTOR HEMBROW
1927
40 × 25 in/101.6 × 63.5 cm

BY THE LATE 1920s the London
General Omnibus Company
had acquired a fleet of luxury
saloon coaches which were
available for private hire.

BOXMOOR

BY MOTOR BUS ROUTE 146
FROM GOLDERS GREEN STATION

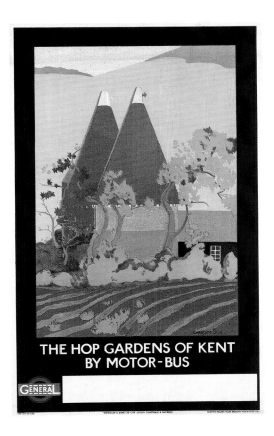

THE HOP GARDENS OF KENT
DOROTHY DIX
1922
40 × 25 in/101.6 × 63.5 cm

BOXMOOR
PADDEN
1921
40 × 25 in/101.6 × 63.5 cm

THREE EXAMPLES by different artists of the brightly coloured, flat treatment of rural landscapes that was so characteristic of travel posters in the 1920s. The Underground began to standardize on the Johnston sans serif typeface at this time, used here on the Boxmoor and Kent posters.

DORKING
F. GREGORY BROWN
1920
30 × 20 in/76.2 × 50.8 cm

New Works
Lightfoot
1932
40 × 25 in/101.6 × 63.5 cm

This image was printed at the top of a blank poster on which details of local new works could be pasted or overprinted. It probably appeared mainly at Piccadilly and District Line stations during the extension and modernization works of 1932–3. At the top right is one of the new, cantilevered, concrete platform shelters designed by Charles Holden: examples can still be seen at Chiswick Park and Stamford Brook stations.

Move to Edgware
William Kermode
1924
40 × 25 in/101.6 × 63.5 cm

NEW WORKS
FRED TAYLOR
1925
40 × 50 in/101.6 × 127 cm

THE HAMPSTEAD TUBE was extended overground from Golders Green to Edgware in 1923–4, prompting new development in what had been open countryside around every station. Fred Taylor's poster makes the point without the need for a single word of copy. A brand new tube station appears at the centre of a bustling suburban building site.

WHY NOT LIVE AT SUDBURY HILL?
CHRISTINE JACKSON
1929
7½ × 4¾ in/19 × 12 cm

REINFORCING the message of many posters of the time, this was one of a series of Underground press advertisements advocating a move to the new suburbs.

KAUFFER'S 'London Museum' is one of his most striking and well-known poster designs. His inspiration was an illuminated model of the Great Fire of 1666 on display in the Museum. This can still be seen, refurbished with new lighting effects and a soundtrack, at the London Museum's successor, the Museum of London, in the Barbican.

LONDON MUSEUM
E. McKNIGHT KAUFFER
1922
40 × 25 in/101.6 × 63.5 cm

MUSEUM OF NATURAL HISTORY
E. McKNIGHT KAUFFER
1923
40 × 25 in/101.6 × 63.5 cm

LONDON MUSEUM
Mondays to Thursdays, & Saturdays 10 a.m.- 4 p.m.
Sundays and Fridays 2 p.m.- 4 p.m.
Admission free (*Tuesdays &*)
                (*Wednesdays & Thursdays 6ᵈ*)
ST JAMES' PARK STATION
Thence a short and pleasant walk across Park

LONDON MUSEUM
REX WHISTLER
1928
40 × 25 in/101.6 × 63.5 cm

THE TATE GALLERY
REX WHISTLER
1928
40 × 25 in/101.6 × 63.5 cm

REX WHISTLER'S POSTER, done in the same year as his mural in the Tate Gallery's restaurant, acts as an advertisement for both the Gallery and the mural. For the poster, he took distinctive elements of the almost surreal, pastiche eighteenth-century mural and wove them into a new composition, adding the two ladies taking tea apparently in the restaurant itself as an extra trompe l'oeil touch.

THE TATE GALLERY
Weekdays 10 a.m.- 4 p.m.
Sundays 2 p.m.- 4 p.m.
Admission free (*Tuesdays and*)
                (*Wednesdays 6ᵈ*)
TRAFALGAR SQ OR WESTMINSTER STN
thence by bus 32, 51, 80, 88, 89, 180 or 181

RUGBY AT TWICKENHAM
LAURA KNIGHT
1921
40 × 25 in/101.6 × 63.5 cm

RUGBY AT TWICKENHAM
BY TRAM
FROM HAMMERSMITH OR SHEPHERDS BUSH

ELECTRIC RAILWAY HOUSE
BROADWAY WESTMINSTER

VINCENT BROOKS DAY & SON. Ltd London W.C.2

742 1000 14 10 21

POSTERS advertising major sporting events were often produced in small panel sizes for use inside Underground cars.

WIMBLEDON TENNIS
ANDRÉ MARTY
1933
9½ × 12¾ in/24 × 32.4 cm

WIMBLEDON
CHARLES BURTON
1930
9½ × 12¾ in/24 × 32.4 cm

CUP FINAL
P. DRAKE BROOKSHAW
1927
11½ × 18¼ in/29.2 × 46.3 cm

UNDERGROUND posters created a glamorous image of London's West End, where there was 'everything for your pleasure', available of course by off-peak travel on the Underground system.

THE WEST-END IS AWAKENING
E. M. DINKEL
1931
40 × 25 in/101.6 × 63.5 cm

TASTING THE RICHES OF LONDON
F. C. HERRICK
1927
40 × 25 in/101.6 × 63.5 cm

TO PANTOMIME AND PLAY
ALMA FAULKNER
1925
40 × 25 in/101.6 × 63.5 cm

THIS POSTER was one of a series illustrating the senses, in which sensual appreciation required the use of a reconstructed Underground symbol.

THE LURE OF THE UNDERGROUND
ALFRED LEETE
1927
40 × 25 in/101.6 × 63.5 cm

THE ARTIST responsible for the most famous of all First World War recruiting posters, showing Lord Kitchener pointing at the viewer with the words 'Your Country Needs You', came up with this humorous approach to Underground advertising. The magnetic lure of the Underground, however, seems to be taking business away from the same company's buses!

OFFICE	HOME
STANISLAUS LONGLEY	**STANISLAUS LONGLEY**
1933	1933
19½ × 12½ in/49.5 × 31.75 cm	19½ × 12½ in/49.5 × 31.75 cm

THESE TWO were part of a series of small panel posters based on the transition from office drudgery to domestic bliss, facilitated by the Underground. The style might be called comic art deco!

WISLEY
ROBERT GIBBINGS
1922
30 × 20 in/76.2 × 50.8 cm

KEW GARDENS
CLIVE GARDINER
1926
40 × 25 in/101.6 × 63.5 cm

KEW GARDENS was a regular subject for Underground posters between the wars; this is a Cubist interpretation of the famous Palm House.

SOME POSTERS contain no travel information, but simply suggest the idea of visiting the countryside with a rural scene and a place name. Wisley in Surrey is well known today as the home of the Royal Horticultural Society's gardens. These would not have been open to day trippers in the 1920s, but the nearby lake, depicted here, is right beside the main London–Guildford road and was easily reached by country bus. The travel connection would probably have been made obvious by displaying the poster on the front panels of buses on either side of the destination boards.

THE PALM HOUSE
KEW GARDENS
BUT SEE IT FOR YOURSELF

BY UNDERGROUND TO
KEW GARDENS
STATION

To Summer Sales
Horace Taylor
1926
40 × 25 in/101.6 × 63.5 cm

THE IMAGERY of the fashion plate and the party invitation are here adapted to the Underground poster and aimed quite specifically at women. Once again, they are an inducement to off-peak travel.

COME OUT OF DOORS IN YOUR
NEW DRESS
ALMA FAULKNER
1928
40 × 25 in/101.6 × 63.5 cm

ON WITH THE DANCE
STANISLAUS LONGLEY
1927
19½ × 12½ in/49.5 × 31.75 cm

WINTER SALES
are best reached by
UNDERGROUND

SUMMER SALES
QUICKLY REACHED BY
UNDERGROUND

KAUFFER'S 'Winter Sales' is the first
example of his move towards abstract
design in his posters. It combines the
influence of traditional Japanese
woodcuts with the dynamic, swirling
lines of Vorticist art, the British
response to Cubism with which Kauffer
was briefly associated.

WINTER SALES
E. MCKNIGHT KAUFFER
1921
40 × 25 in/101.6 × 63.5 cm

SUMMER SALES
MARY KOOP
1925
40 × 25 in/101.6 × 63.5 cm

NO WET, NO COLD
MANNER
1929
40 × 25 in/101.6 × 63.5 cm

LONDON'S UMBRELLA
F. C. HERRICK
1925
40 × 25 in/101.6 × 63.5 cm

THE BRIGHT red vehicles of the London General Omnibus Company made only rare appearances in the landscapes of the poster artists. Open-top buses were already being replaced by the late 1920s, but they convey a suitably summery feel to these images. 'General Joy' is, of course, a deliberate pun on the company name.

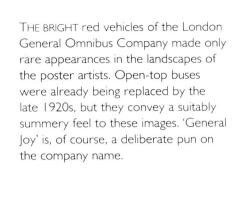

RIDE GENERAL AND RIDE WELL

RIDE GENERAL AND RIDE WELL
J. H. DOWD
1926
40 × 25 in/101.6 × 63.5 cm

MEALS TASTE BETTER OUT-OF-DOORS
AUSTIN COOPER
1928
40 × 25 in/101.6 × 63.5 cm

SUMMER OUTINGS BY PRIVATE BUS
L. B. BLACK
1926
30 × 20 in/76.2 × 50.8 cm

MEALS TASTE BETTER OUT-OF-DOORS

WHAT ABOUT IT ?
GENERAL **FOR SURE**

**SUMMER OUTINGS
BY PRIVATE BUS**
RIDE GENERAL AND RIDE WELL

GENERAL JOY
VERA WILLOUGHBY
1928
40 × 25 in/10 .6 × 63.5 cm

KEW

RICHMOND

KINGSTON

HAMPTON
COURT

WEYBRIDGE

CHERTSEY

STAINES

WINDSOR

NOW IS THE SEASON OF THE YEAR TO LEAVE THE STUFFY TOWN, AND IN THE
COOL OF THE EVENING SEEK OUT A FRESH AND AIRY SPACE FOR PLEASURE
BY LONDON'S UNDERGROUND.

NOW IS THE SEASON OF THE YEAR
C. R. W. NEVINSON
1925
64 40 × 50 in/101.6 × 127 cm

BRIGHTER LONDON
FOR THEATRELAND
TRAVEL BY
UNDERGROUND

FOR THEATRELAND
H. S. WILLIAMSON
1924
40 × 25 in/101.6 × 63.5 cm

THEATRES and cinemas bought extensive advertising space on buses and station platforms. The Underground's own posters therefore encouraged these entertainment activities, while taking care not to give free promotion to any individual venues.

The Film-lover travels UNDERGROUND

Piccadilly, Oxford Circus, Leicester Square, Strand Stations

THE FILM-LOVER
CHARLES PEARS
1930
40 × 25 in/101.6 × 63.5 cm

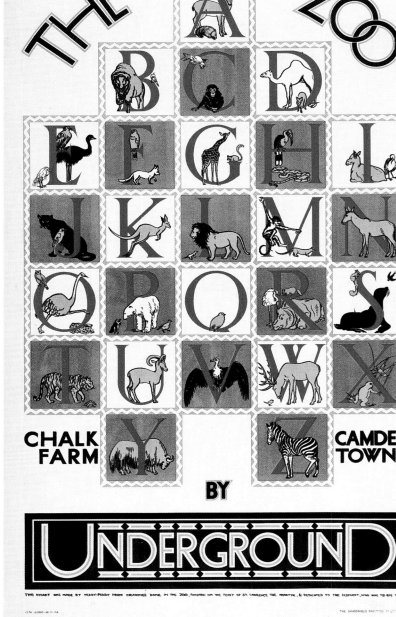

FOR THE ZOO
DOROTHY BURROUGHES
1922
40 × 25 in/101.6 × 63.5 cm

THE ZOO ALPHABET
HERRY-PERRY
1928
40 × 25 in/101.6 × 63.5 cm

THE LONDON ZOO features on more Underground posters than any other subject; at least two per year were produced throughout the 1920s. This was certainly a case of free advertising, but it offered enormous scope for artists to vary their subject matter. The irony is that the Zoo is not actually on the Underground, and is a long walk from either Regent's Park or Camden Town stations.

FOR THE ZOO

Book to REGENT'S PARK or CAMDEN TOWN

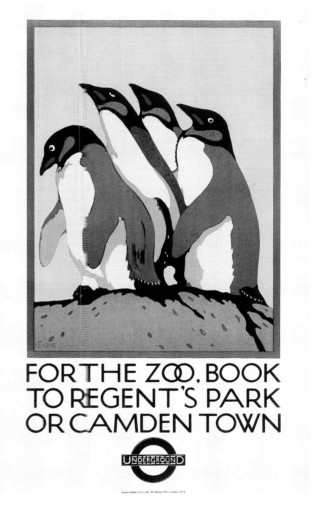

For the Zoo
Ruth Sandys
1925
40 × 25 in/101.6 × 63.5 cm

For the Zoo
Charles Paine
1921
40 × 25 in/101.6 × 63.5 cm

THESE FOUR posters show the full influence of Modernism on poster art, with the use of bold geometric shapes and lettering as an integral part of the design. The Underground did not always insist on the use of the Johnston typeface at this time. Kauffer, in particular, used some of the new typographical styles pioneered by the Bauhaus School in Germany. Fletcher's design suggests a compromise on the typography, with Johnston at the bottom, but the main heading in a traditional serif face which sits rather inappropriately with the Modernist illustration.

SHOP BETWEEN TEN AND FOUR
FLETCHER
1926
40 × 25 in/101.6 × 63.5 cm

POWER
E. McKnight Kauffer
1931
40 × 25 in/101.6 × 63.5 cm

PLAY BETWEEN SIX AND TWELVE
E. McKnight Kauffer
1930
40 × 25 in/101.6 × 63.5 cm

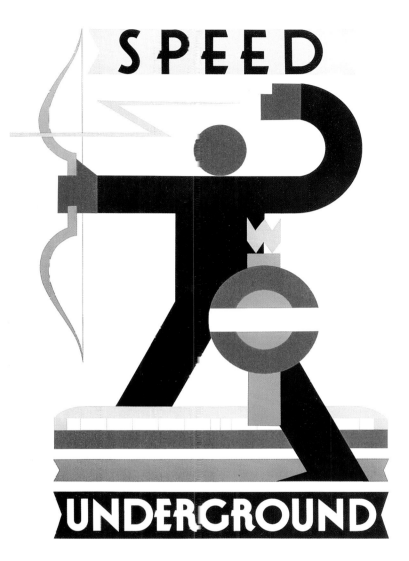

SPEED
Alan Rogers
1930
40 × 25 n/101.6 × 63.5 cm

TO THE CONCERT HALLS
AUBREY HAMMOND
1923
40 × 25 in/101.6 × 63.5 cm

BRIGHTEST LONDON
AND HOME BY
UNDERGROUND

BRIGHTEST LONDON
HORACE TAYLOR
1924
40 × 25 in/101.6 × 63.5 cm

Q.E.D.
MARGARET CALKIN JAMES
1929
40 × 25 in/101.6 × 63.5 cm

FRANK PICK always justified advertising that was slightly above people's heads as being preferable to a descent to the lowest common denominator. A good poster, he believed, could be both inspirational and aspirational; images populated largely by the fashionable and wealthy were not, therefore, aimed at those people alone. However, his dictum that the message must remain comprehensible to the 'man in the street' is possibly compromised by 'Q.E.D.', which assumes in the viewer a basic knowledge of Latin tags. *Quod Erat Demonstrandum* means 'which was to be demonstrated' – in this case the apparently obvious contention that smart people attending a show in town *always* travel by tube!

BRIGHTEST LONDON
HORACE TAYLOR
1924
40 × 25 in/101.6 × 63.5 cm

INTERNATIONAL ADVERTISING
EXHIBITION
F. C. HERRICK
1920
40 × 50 in/101.6 × 127 cm

HERRICK'S first poster for the Underground featured a range of advertising characters, some of whom are still in use today. They include the Michelin Man and the HMV ('His Master's Voice') dog (left), the Bisto Kids (foreground), Mr Punch and Johnnie Walker (centre, middle distance) and the Kodak girl (right). The Underground and the General each had a stand at the International Advertising Exhibition to encourage advertisers to make more use of the promotional space available on stations, buses and trains.

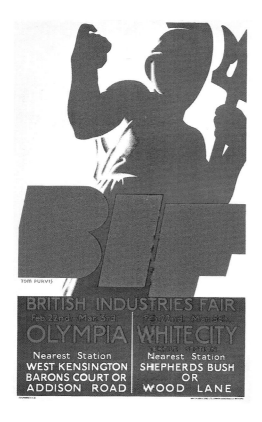

BRITISH INDUSTRIES FAIR
TOM PURVIS
1932
20¼ × 8½ in/51.4 × 21.6 cm

TOM PURVIS was one of the major
British poster artists of the inter-war
years but, surprisingly, he was
commissioned to do only three designs
for the Underground.

RAF DISPLAY
DORA BATTY
1932
10 × 13 in/25.4 × 33 cm

THE ANNUAL display by the Royal Air
Force at Hendon aerodrome always
attracted large crowds, most of them
arriving by tube at Colindale station.
Unfortunately, the RAF's fleet of
bi-planes hardly matched up to the
image of elegant modernity suggested
by Dora Batty's poster.

HAMPTON COURT BY TRAM

HAMPTON COURT
ALDO COSOMATI
1923
30 × 20 in/76.2 × 50.8 cm

BY TRAM TO HAMPTON COURT

HAMPTON COURT
DOROTHY PATON
1927
30 × 20 in/76.2 × 50.8 cm

TWO ERAS in the history of Hampton Court as a royal palace: Aldo Cosomati depicts the Tudor façade in silhouette, dominated by the figure of King Henry VIII, who seized the palace from Cardinal Wolsey in 1529 and enlarged it for his own use. Dorothy Paton's view shows a later part of the palace, the façade built in the 1690s by Christopher Wren for William and Mary. Getting to Hampton Court by tram would have been rather a slow business unless your journey began in West London. The quickest route from central London was by Southern Railway from Waterloo, but the Underground would naturally have kept quiet about that.

DERBY DAY
HERRY-PERRY
1928
9½ × 12¾ in/24 × 32.4 cm

HERRY-PERRY'S design is a witty adaptation of Paolo Uccello's famous fifteenth-century painting of mounted knights in combat at the Battle of San Romano, which hangs in the National Gallery in London. The joke is acknowledged with an 'apology' printed in the bottom right-hand corner of the poster.

TROOPING THE COLOUR
MARGARET CALKIN JAMES
1932
16 × 12½ in/40.6 × 31.75 cm

ROYAL TOURNAMENT OLYMPIA
CHARLES BURTON
1930
10 × 12 in/25.4 × 30.5 cm

THANKS TO THE

UNDERGROUND

ZERO

THANKS TO THE
UNDERGROUND
ZERO (HANS SCHLEGER)
1935
40 × 25 in/101.6 × 63.5 cm

THE ARTISTIC range of London
Transport's posters was
enriched in the 1930s by a
number of commissions from
internationally known designers.
Hans Schleger, 'Zero', was a
refugee from Nazi Germany.

4 IN 1933 A NEW ORGANIZATION, the London Passenger Transport Board, was created to run al. bus, tram and underground railway services in the capital. London Transport, as the new authority was soon generally known, took over the Underground Group of companies. the various council tramway systems, the

Metropolitan Ra lway and all the small independent bus companies. For the first time it was possible to plan and co-ordinate the development of public transport in London through one body. With Pick as Chief Executive of London Transport, the high standard of the Underground Group's poster publicity was maintained and extended to cover all elements of the newly enlarged system.

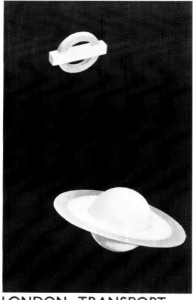

LONDON TRANSPORT-

LONDON TRANSPORT – KEEPS LONDON GOING
MAN RAY
1939
40 × 25 in/101.6 × 63.5 cm
(one of a pair)

THE AMERICAN Man Ray probably designec this pair poster while on a visit from Paris. Like Schleger, he took the familiar bar and circle symbol as his starting point and translated it into an unfamiliar context.

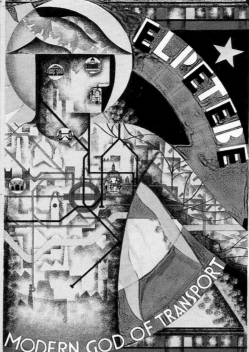

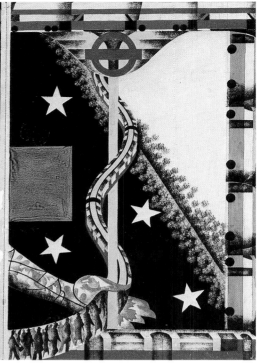

LPTB MODERN GOD OF TRANSPORT
LILIAN DRING
c. 1933
14½ × 29½ in/36.8 × 74.9 cm
[Never printed]

THE NEW transport authority, the London Passenger Transport Board, is portrayed here as a modern Mercury, messenger of the gods. His heart is the London Transport symbol, with the Underground lines as his arteries and a tube train forming the snake on his rod. Various appropriate London landmarks act as his features: his mouth is the BBC Broadcasting House, his eyes the National Gallery, his ears the Albert Hall and his throat Tower Bridge. Lilian Dring's ambitious design for a triple poster was sent unsolicited to Frank Pick. Apparently he was impressed, but told her that he 'dared not' use it because of the cost.

THE UNDERGROUND BRINGS ALL GOOD THINGS NEARER
DORA BATTY
1933
40 × 25 in/101.6 × 63.5 cm

ANOTHER classical allusion employs Mercury again, this time in more conventional guise bringing Persephone with her horn of plenty back from the Underworld/Underground.

REGATTA-TIME'S PLEASANT
JEAN DUPAS
1933
40 × 25 in/101.6 × 63.5 cm

THE WINGED LPTB symbol, designed by
C. W. Bacon, can be seen here in the
bottom right-hand corner, in one of its
few appearances. It was not popular
and, within a few months, the
Underground's bar and circle device
was reinstated as London Transport's
main graphic symbol.

"Regatta-time's pleasant
Thrice pleasant in laughing July."

Richmond Station for the River

SPRING CALLING
LONDON LISTENING
KEITH HENDERSON
1935
40 × 25 in/101.6 × 63.5 cm (each poster)

THIS EARLY example of a pair poster
has two 'double royal' size posters
placed together to form a continuous
graphic design.

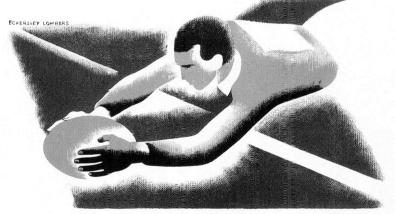

THIRD TEST MATCH, THE OVAL
CLIFFORD AND ROSEMARY ELLIS
1939
10 × 12 in/25.4 × 30.5 cm

RUGBY LEAGUE FINAL
ECKERSLEY LOMBERS
1938
10 × 12 in/25.4 × 30.5 cm

THE PROUD CITY

CHELSEA POWER HOUSE FROM MEEK STREET

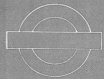

"...the poor buildings lose themselves in the dim sky, and the tall chimneys become campanili, and the warehouses are palaces in the night, and the whole city hangs in the heavens..."

James McNeill Whistler

THE PROUD CITY
WALTER SPRADBERY
1944
40 × 25 in/101.6 × 63.5 cm

LONDON TRANSPORT'S power station at Chelsea is silhouetted against wartime searchlights and surrounded by the devastation of the Blitz.

5

THE SECOND WORLD WAR had an immediate impact on civilian life in London. Unnecessary travel was discouraged and publicity posters ceased completely only a few months after the war began. The main role for pictoral posters was now to provide information and, increasingly, to boost the morale of

both passengers and staff in extremely difficult conditions. Due to shortage of paper, fewer posters were issued and most of them appeared in a reduced size. As well as maintaining a service throughout the Blitz of 1940-1, London Transport provided improvized air-raid shelters for thousands of Londoners in its deep-level tube stations.

THE PROUD CITY
WALTER SPRADBERY
1944
40 × 25 in/101.6 × 63.5 cm

This series of six posters celebrated London's survival during the Blitz. They were intended to convey, in the artist's own words, 'the sense that havoc itself is passing and with new days come new hopes'.

BACK ROOM BOYS – THEY ALSO SERVE
FRED TAYLOR
1942
24½ × 20 in/62.2 × 50.8 cm (each poster)

FROM A SERIES of eight morale-boosting posters, five examples highlight the role of the staff behind the scenes, whose essential maintenance and repair work kept the system running in difficult wartime conditions. Many of these workers, of course, were women, which lends the series title a certain irony. The layout, with a central image framed by an illustrated border, is similar to A. S. Hartrick's First World War series 'Playing the Game' (see pages 40–41).

CABLE MAINTENANCE

'THEY ALSO SERVE'

BOILER MAINTENANCE

'THEY ALSO SERVE'

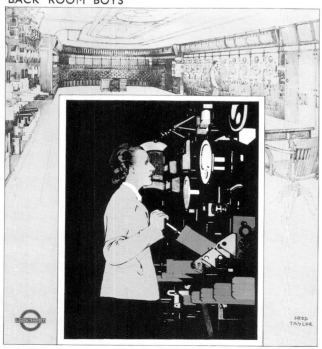

POWER CONTROL

'THEY ALSO SERVE'

BUS MAINTENANCE

'THEY ALSO SERVE'

Please pass down the car?

___ SOMEDAY YOU MIGHT
WANT TO GET IN, YOURSELF!

PLEASE STAND ON THE RIGHT
OF THE ESCALATOR

A FOUGASSE is a small land-mine, an appropriate pseudonym for cartoonist Cyril Kenneth Bird, who adopted it when he was a Royal Engineer in the First World War. His humorous public information posters are some of the best-remembered graphic images of the Second World War.

PLEASE PASS DOWN THE CAR
PLEASE PASS ALONG THE PLATFORM
PLEASE HAVE YOUR TICKET READY AT THE BARRIER
PLEASE STAND ON THE RIGHT OF THE ESCALATOR
FOUGASSE
1944
24½ × 19¼ in/62.2 × 48.9 cm (each poster)

"Isn't it lucky I'm not in a hurry?"

PLEASE HAVE YOUR TICKET
READY AT THE BARRIER

The more we are together, the more uncomfortable we'll be.

PLEASE PASS ALONG THE
PLATFORM

Pilot, all alone you ride,
Through the bowels of the town.
Up into the black outside
Where the bombs are whistling down.

Bombs and blizzards, fogs and frights —
"Dead man's handle" at your breast —
Lights — and lights — for over Lights —
On you ride and never rest.

On to Barking, on to Kew!
Master of a trying trade,
Seldom do we think of you,
Never do we feel afraid.

A. P. Herbert

Thank you, Mrs. Porter,
For a good job stoutly done;
Your voice is clear, and the Hun can hear
When you cry "South Kensington!"

The world must hurry homeward,
The soldier on his way,
And the wheels whizz round on the Underground
At the voice of the girls in grey.

And though the skies are noisy
How calm the voices are —
"Upminster train! That man again!
Pass further down the car!"

A. P. Herbert

How proud upon your quarterdeck you stand,
Conductor — Captain — of the mighty bus!
Like some Columbus you survey the Strand,
A calm newcomer in a sea of fuss.

You may be tired — how cheerfully you clip.
Clip in the dark, with one eye on the street —
Two decks — one pair of legs — a rolling ship —
Much on your mind — and fat men on your feet!

The sirens blow, and death is in the air.
Still at her post the trusty Captain stands,
And counts her change, and scampers up the stair
As brave a sailor as the King commands.

A. P. Herbert

SEEING IT THROUGH
ERIC KENNINGTON
1944
44 × 31¼ in/111.8 × 79.4 cm
(each poster)

THE SERIES 'Seeing It Through' commemorated the everyday heroism of civilian workers in wartime. The sitters for Eric Kennington's portraits, from which the posters were taken, were all members of London Transport's staff and not professional models. Frank Clark, the motorman, was injured when his train was hit in a bombing raid at Sloane Square, but managed to lead his passengers to safety. Elsie Birrell of Stockwell station was one of the first woman porters to be recruited in 1940. Mrs M. J. Morgan, a clippie from Athol Street garage in Poplar, saved four children in an air raid by pushing them under the seats of her bus.

ENJOY YOUR WAR WORK
ARTIST UNKNOWN
1941
40 × 25 in/101.6 × 63.5 cm

The Spirit of 1943

THE SPIRIT OF 1943
L. D. LUARD
1943
24½ × 19¾ in/62.2 × 50.2 cm

OUR HERITAGE
ROBERT AUSTIN
1943
24½ × 19¾ in/62.2 × 50.2 cm

AUSTIN'S portrait of Britain's wartime prime minister, with an extract from the most defiant of his parliamentary speeches, was one of a series depicting individuals who had successfully defended the country in crisis, including Drake and Nelson.

OUR HERITAGE

Printed for the passengers and staff of London Transport to recall other occasions of the nation's will and high purpose.

AUSTIN - 1943

We shall go on to the end, we shall fight in France, we shall fight on the seas and oceans, we shall fight with growing confidence and growing strength in the air, we shall defend our island, whatever the cost may be, we shall fight on the beaches, we shall fight on the landing grounds, we shall fight in the fields and in the streets, we shall fight in the hills; we shall never surrender . . . until, in God's good time, the new world, with all its power and might, steps forth to the rescue and the liberation of the old.

The Rt. Hon. WINSTON S. CHURCHILL, P.C., M.P., after the collapse of France, June, 1940

ROYAL LONDON
BUCKINGHAM PALACE
JOHN BAINBRIDGE
1953
40 × 25 in/101.6 × 63.5 cm
(each poster)

6 LONDON TRANSPORT CARRIED more passengers in the late 1940s than ever before. The Pick tradition of commissioning pictorial poster publicity was revived, but on a reduced scale, and after a promising start the new campaign began to lose its impetus in the 1950s. In comparison with the pre-war years, the posters seem limited

in range, reflecting an apparent shortage of talented young graphic artists. Poster art, unable to stem the decline in passenger numbers in the 1950s, was viewed as an outdated publicity medium.

A NUMBER of London Transport posters had a royal theme in Coronation year: Queen Elizabeth II was crowned on 2 June 1953.

CITY

stone and city brick is London's history for all to see. You can see the City best when its workday inhabitants have deserted it. On a Saturday afternoon or Sunday Wren and his peers are very much alone in their glory. There is time and space to stand and admire, to snap or sketch, to look above the busline, and in one small square mile seek and find treasure which The Bank can never value . . .

Some suggestions for Citygoers (who may or may not know their City)

ALL HALLOWS BARKING BY THE TOWER
A pre-Great Fire Church, now the shrine of Toc H's parent Lamp of Maintenance. Its crypt museum takes you back to Roman and Saxon London.
District and Circle Lines to Tower Hill.

ST. BARTHOLOMEW THE GREAT
Outside the Tudor gatehouse the boy King Richard II faced the Peasants' Revolt in 1381. The Church has London's finest Norman interior with a charming 14th-century Lady Chapel and the tomb of Rahere, the 12th-century founder of 'Bart's' Hospital over the way.
Circle and Metropolitan Lines to Aldersgate (closed on Sundays) or Farringdon; or Central Line to St. Paul's.
Bus 4A to Aldersgate Station; bus 63 or Holborn Circus trolleybuses to Charterhouse Street; trolleybuses 567, 677, 679 to Smithfield; or buses along Holborn Viaduct to Old Bailey.

GOUGH SQUARE
The City as it was in the 18th century. At No. 17 is the attic study where Dr. Johnson compiled much of his Dictionary. 'When a man is tired of London' said the Doctor, 'he is tired of life'.
Open weekdays from 10.30 a.m. to 4.30 p.m. from September to April. Closed Sundays and Bank Holidays. Admission 1/.
District and Circle Lines to Blackfriars, or Piccadilly Line to Aldwych (closed on Sundays).
Through Hind Court from Fleet Street.
Buses along Fleet Street to the Daily Telegraph building.

GUILDHALL
The war-battered 15th-century Great Hall is still worth seeing, and the Eastern Crypt is a fine example of groined vaulting. The Museum is rich in City antiquities, the Library in London prints, and there is usually an exhibition in the Art Gallery.
Open Mondays to Fridays from 10 a.m. to 5 p.m., Saturdays 10 a.m. to 4 p.m. Closed Sundays. Admission free.
Central and Northern Lines to Bank, or District and Circle Lines to Mansion House.
Buses along Cheapside or Moorgate.

ST. MARY-LE-BOW
Having admired Wren's loveliest spire turn west and capture (while you can) a view of St. Paul's revealed by the blitz that destroyed those 'Bow Bells' which used to define the true cockney.
District and Circle Lines to Mansion House, or Central and Northern Lines to Bank.
Buses along Cheapside.

THE MONUMENT
To see Wren's spires to perfection climb the 311 steps inside the Monument. It was erected to a modified Wren design to commemorate the origin of the Great Fire (1666) in Pudding Lane nearby.
Open weekdays 9 a.m. to 4 p.m., from October to the end of March. Closed Sundays. Admission 6d.
District and Circle Lines to Monument (escalator connection from Central and Northern Lines at Bank).
All buses which cross London Bridge.

THE ROYAL EXCHANGE
Walk on the stones trod by its Elizabethan founder, Sir Thomas Gresham (whose grasshopper surmounts the eastern cupola), and study London's history in the paintings along the arcaded walls.
Open Mondays to Fridays from 10 a.m. to 5 p.m., Saturdays from 10 a.m. to midday. Admission free.
Central and Northern Lines to Bank (escalator connection from District and Circle Lines at Monument).
Buses to The Bank.

THE TEMPLE
Read the history of the Knights Templar, go hand in hand with Elia, stroll the Georgian terraces and feed the birds in Fountain Court, but be sure to go inside Middle Temple Hall—the Elizabethan screen, the original glass and Drake's table survive.
Open Mondays to Fridays from 10 a.m. to midday and from 3 p.m. to 4.30 p.m., on Saturdays from 10 a.m. to 5 p.m. Closed Sundays. Admission free.
District and Circle Lines to Temple, or Piccadilly Line to Aldwych (closed on Sundays).
Buses along Fleet Street or Victoria Embankment.

THE TOWER
There is more, far more, here than the Regalia and the Bloody Tower which were your delight as a child. This time you can admire the exquisite Norman Chapel of St. John, study one of the best Armouries in England, and enjoy London's River from the Terrace.
Open on weekdays from 9 a.m. to 4 p.m. from October to April. Closed on Sundays. Admission 1/. Children 6d. Free on Saturdays and Bank Holidays.
District and Circle Lines to Tower Hill.
Buses 42, 78 to Tower Gardens.

by LONDON TRANSPORT

CITY
EDWARD BAWDEN
1952
40 × 25 in/101.6 × 63.5 cm (each poster)

BAWDEN'S assemblage of architectural images from the City's square mile includes the Old Bailey (top left), the Monument (top right), St Paul's Cathedral, Tower Bridge and Leadenhall Market (lower right). The London pigeon from his pre-war poster of St James's Park (see page 83) reappears in slimmed down form, sporting the London Transport logo as an eye

LONDON ROVERS
PETER ROBERSON
1958
40 × 25 in/101.6 × 63.5 cm

ONE-DAY ROVER tickets, the
forerunners of today's Travelcards,
were introduced in the late 1950s. For
five shillings a Red or Green Rover
gave travellers the freedom of all the
central area or country bus routes,
outside the peak hours. The Twin
Rover at eight shillings and sixpence
combined the Underground with
central area buses. Unfortunately, at
about the time this poster appeared
London was in the grip of its worst
ever bus strike, which lasted for seven
weeks.

'The height and spread of frontage shining sheer
The quiring signs, the rejoicing roofs and spires –
'Tis El Dorado – El Dorado plain
The Golden City . . .'   Can you identify this quotation?

Two TWIN ROVER tickets will be sent to each of the first ten applicants to name correctly the
author and the poem from which it is taken. Postcards please to the Publicity Officer, 55 Broadway, S.W.1.

WINTER LONDON
PICCADILLY CIRCUS
MOLLY MOSS
1950
40 × 25 in/101.6 × 63.5 cm (one of a pair)

LONDON'S FAIRS
WILLIAM ROBERTS
1951
40 × 25 in/101.6 × 63.5 cm (one of a pair)

PAIR POSTERS gave both the artist and the copywriter more space to develop their contributions to the final design. A larger pictorial image, uncluttered by title or text, was paired with a second poster of the same size carrying quite long descriptive copy and detailed travel information, often with a decorative border to match.

TWO IMPRESSIONS of the Thames show it as a working river before the decline of the Port of London in the 1960s. The picturesque pre-war paddle-steamers of the Woolwich free ferry were replaced by diesel-engined craft in 1963. Soon afterwards the cranes and lighters began to disappear from the Pool of London. Apart from the bridges, the only features of John Minton's river scenes which survive today are a few of the old warehouses, now mostly converted into luxury apartments.

WOOLWICH FERRY
BETTY SWANWICK
1949
40 × 25 in/101.6 × 63.5 cm (one of a pair)

THE ZOO AQUARIUM
ENID MARX
1957
40 × 25 in/101.6 × 63.5 cm (one of a pair)

AS WELL AS this pa r poster, Enid Marx designed woollen moquette seating for Underground trains in the 1930s and 1940s.

Old Noah stocked his sturdy Ark
With animals both old and gnu
And sailed away to Regent's Park
To found a comprehensive Zoo.

To Whipsnade, then, the course was clear
For Shem the navigator,
To start one in the open air
Ideal for the spectator.

The booklet 'How to Get There' cites
Admission fees and when to go
To Zoos and all the other sights
The London visitor should know.

The best way to the Zoo at Regent's Park is to go by Underground to Camden Town or Baker Street and take a 74 bus to the gate. The best way to Whipsnade is to take a 726 Green Line coach from Baker Street (Allsop Place, just behind the station) direct to the gate. The single fare to Whipsnade is 4/3.

'How to Get There' is a London Transport booklet which lists some 400 of London's places of interest, both famous and less well-known, together with times of opening, prices of admission and how to get there by London Transport. 'How to Get There' is included free with the guide-book 'Visitor's London' which costs 4/6. It can also be bought separately, price 6d. All London Transport publications, including free maps and leaflets, can be obtained from the Publicity Officer, London Transport, 55 Broadway, Westminster, S.W.I.

LONDON'S RIVER

The Thames is a gateway on the world, sweeping into London from the Nore with a tide of white gulls to remind the Londoner of his heritage. But in providing a highway to the far oceans for the docks and warehouses the river gives London not only its greatness but much of its beauty.

He who pauses on one of its many bridges can see the silver grey City rising above the sparkling water, he can discover the full majesty of St. Paul's above unexpected masts. He can watch the busy traffic of the river, the tugs with their broken necklaces of barges, dipping their funnels as they pass beneath. And he can enjoy the pleasure of a trip on the river—downstream through the Pool to the seaward shipping, or upstream, all urgency forgotten, curving among the meadows into the heart of England.

SOME THAMES BRIDGES

TOWER
By train to Tower Hill
By bus 42, 78

LONDON
By train to London Bridge
or Monument
By bus or tram to London Bridge

WATERLOO (For South Bank Exhibition)
By train to Waterloo
By bus or tram to Waterloo
or Victoria Embankment

HUNGERFORD (Foot)
For Roy. Festival Hall
By train to Charing Cross
By bus or tram to Victoria Embankment

BAILEY (Foot)
(For South Bank Exhibition only)
By train to Charing Cross
By bus or tram to Victoria Embankment

WESTMINSTER
By train to Westminster
By bus or tram to County Hall or
Bridge Street, Westminster

CHELSEA
For Festival Pleasure Gardens, Battersea
By train to Sloane Square, thence bus 137

ALBERT
For Festival Pleasure Gardens, Battersea
By train to Victoria, thence bus 39

BATTERSEA
By train to Sloane Square, thence bus 19
By bus 19, 39, 49, 49

PUTNEY
By train to Putney Bridge
By bus 14, *14a, 22, 30, 74, 85, 93, 96
By trolleybus 628, 630

HAMMERSMITH
By train to Hammersmith
By trolleybus 628, 630, 655, 660, 667

KEW
By train to Gunnersbury thence bus *27,
71, *27b or trolleybus 655, 657, 667
By bus 17, *33, *27, 27a, *27b, 65, 65a,
*91, *112
By trolleybus 655, 657, 667

RICHMOND
By train to Richmond
By bus *27, 27a, *27b, †33, 37, 65, 65a,
71, 73, 90, 90b, †211, *112
By Green Line 714, 716, 717

KINGSTON
By train to Richmond thence bus 65,
65a, 71, *112; or to Putney Bridge
thence bus 85
By Green Line 714, 716, 717, 718

HAMPTON COURT
By train to Hammersmith thence bus
*27b, trolleybus 667; or to Wimbledon,
thence trolleybus 604
By Green Line 716, 717, 718

CHERTSEY
By Green Line 716

STAINES
By Green Line 701, 702, 718

WINDSOR
By Green Line 704, 705, 718

† Weekdays only   * Sundays only   § Saturdays and Sunday only

BY LONDON TRANSPORT

LONDON'S RIVER
JOHN MINTON
1951
40 × 25 in/101.6 × 63.5 cm (each poster)

HANS UNGER received his first commission from London Transport in 1950, and designed more than fifty posters over the next twenty years. 'Village Life', a pair poster, was Len Deighton's only design for London Transport as a graphic artist. He became a successful writer, beginning with his best-selling espionage novel *The Ipcress File* in 1962.

WINTER – COUNTRY WALKS
HANS UNGER
1958
40 × 25 in/101.6 × 63.5 cm

LONDON'S COUNTRY
VILLAGE LIFE
LEN DEIGHTON
1957
40 × 25 in/101.6 × 63.5 cm (one of a pair)

COUNTRY MARKETS
PHILIP ROBERTS
1960
40 × 25 in/101.6 × 63.5 cm

EILLINGSGATE

Pay a pre-breakfast visit. No 'Billingsgate compliments'' today, but the tradition of salty exchanges persists, leather hats are in evidence, and porters' heads still support nonchalant hundredweights. The rainbow harvest, ice-stiff in boxes or stranded on the slab, brings a deep-sea tang to London's doorstep.

Richard Beston, 1854.
Underground to Monument.

COVENT GARDEN

Another early morning expedition. Chaos is the order of the day, merchant and customer bargain in a vegetable shorthand which defeats the uninitiated ear, porters battle through the throng between mountains of begonias and broccoli, grapefruit and greens. Try not to obstruct—here time is money, and neither grows on trees.

Underground to Covent Garden.

LONDON MARKETS

Explore London's rich variety of markets. You may not want a peck of peppers, you may not unearth a Ming vase. What you will surely find is a precious amalgam of uncompromising good humour, tolerance and unquenchable vitality that is the very stuff of working London.

LONDON MARKETS
GAYNOR CHAPMAN
1961
40 × 25 in/101.6 × 63.5 cm

ANY country market will provide you with colour, entertainment, education and possibly a bargain— a day in the fresh air with an excuse for pottering. . .

A new leaflet 'COUNTRY MARKETS' lists those near London showing the days they open and how to get there. It is free, from the Travel Enquiry Offices at St. James's Park and Piccadilly Circus Underground Stations, or at the City Information Centre, St. Paul's Churchyard. Or write for your copy to the Publicity Officer, London Transport, 280 Marylebone Road, N.W.1.

115

LONDON AFTER DARK

In the dusk, the West End comes to life. Street lamps brighten, and the twinkling lights turn Piccadilly Circus into a brashly magical fairyland. Floodlighting lends to St. Paul's, the National Gallery, Westminster Abbey, a silvery, sharp-etched clarity. Evening shopping (on Thursdays), theatres, cinemas, concerts, restaurants—London Transport takes you there, and home again. Buses run late, and the Underground until after midnight—23 30 on Sundays.

Travel Enquiries: telephone 01-222 1234 at any time, day or night.

LONDON AFTER DARK
FRED MILLETT
1968
40 × 25 in/101.6 × 63.5 cm

FRED MILLETT'S collage was one of London Transport's few ventures into Pop Art in the 1960s.

7 IN 1963 CONSTRUCTION WORK BEGAN on the Victoria Line, the first new tube railway to be built under central London for over fifty years. But modernization and new developments in the 1960s and 1970s were accompanied by problems and setbacks; financial difficulties, staff shortages, unreliability and a decline in

1963-84

passenger numbers. Art poster publicity became widely regarded as an irrelevant luxury: direct commissions to artists were cut back from about six posters a year in the 1960s to virtually none in the late 1970s. Meanwhile publicity posters were contracted out to agencies, who tended to use photographic images rather than artworks: these rarely matched the innovation and variety of previous campaigns.

ROUND LONDON SIGHTSEEING TOUR
ABRAM GAMES
1971
40 × 25 in/101.6 × 63.5 cm

THIS BOLD contemporary image was commissioned from one of the leading graphic designers of the time. Abram Games designed his first poster for London Transport in 1937.

LONDON ZOO
ABRAM GAMES
1976
40 × 25 in/101.6 × 63.5 cm

THIS WAS THE LAST poster designed by
Abram Games in forty years of
working for London Transport. It is
thought by many to be his best.

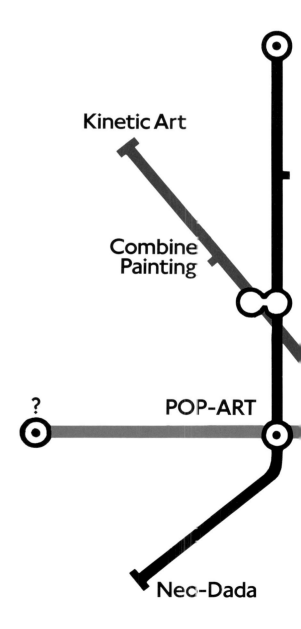

Kinetic Art

Combine
Painting

?

POP-ART

Neo-Dada

ART TODAY The Tate, re-hung with taste and logic, offers the academically approved, the Whitechapel the young and middle-generation painters. The Greater London Council sets contemporary British sculpture against the simpler pleasures of Battersea Park. Complete your survey with the commercial galleries of deepest Mayfair and Chelsea, and the avant-garde extremes. For all these new frontiers, the explorer's kit is simple—an open mind, Underground and bus maps, and a sense of humour. For The Tate Gallery: Underground or bus to Westminster, then bus 77B. For The Whitechapel Art Gallery: Underground to Aldgate East. For Battersea Park: Underground to Sloane Square, then by bus 137.

ART TODAY
HANS UNGER
1966
40 × 25 in/101.6 × 63.5 cm

FEMME BIEN INFORMÉE
HARRY STEVENS
1972
40 × 25 in/101.6 × 63.5 cm

TWO ARTISTS make visually witty comments on modern art; the 'master' in Harry Stevens' subtitle is of course Picasso.

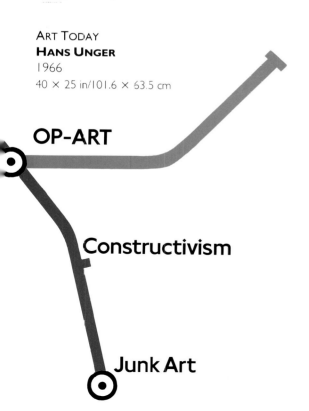

OP-ART

Constructivism

Junk Art

119

COVENT GARDEN, London's main wholesale fruit, vegetable and flower market, was transferred to a new site south of the River Thames at Nine Elms in 1974. The original nineteenth-century market buildings shown in John Griffiths' poster were then renovated for new uses as shops, restaurants, museums and a sports hall in the 1980s. The main building depicted in the poster is the old Flower Market, now the home of the London Transport Museum.

RHUBARB AND ROSES, sweet peas and prima donnas, mingle in glorious confusion at Covent Garden. At six in the morning this great market is a dazzling sight. In the quiet of evening, fashionable shoes pick their way through vegetable remnants towards Bellini, Verdi or Mozart. At the western end stands St. Paul's Church, Inigo Jones's 'handsomest barn in England'; pillared, imposing, and confusingly back-to-front.

Underground to Covent Garden

VICTORIAN LONDON
Victorian architecture expressed the powerful, sometimes grandiose, aspirations of a rich, expanding empire, confidently unaware of the precariousness of its foundations. Victorian London is a heritage in jeopardy, and irreplaceable. A new London Transport publication, prepared with the help of the Victorian Society, offers a very brief survey, lists some examples, and suggests how to get there by bus or Underground. Price 5p at London Transport Travel Enquiry offices.

RHUBARB AND ROSES
JOHN GRIFFITHS
1965
40 × 25 in/101.6 × 63.5 cm

VICTORIAN LONDON
DAVID GENTLEMAN
1974
40 × 25 in/101.6 × 63.5 cm

THE BUILDINGS of Christopher Wren are here interpreted in different media. The St Paul's poster is taken from a conventional flat artwork, but the Christopher Wren design is a photograph of an elaborate three-dimensional paper sculpture of the architect and a selection of his city churches.

O LD ST PAUL'S — old because the West Front has lately been transformed. If you have ever thought London soot can beautify, go at once and look at St Paul's from the top of Ludgate Hill. Imagine the whole building as Wren himself saw it, and then make a contribution, lordly or modest, to the Lord Mayor's fund for a complete transformation.

OLD ST PAUL'S
ANTHONY ECKERSLEY
1964
40 × 25 in/101.6 × 63.5 cm

SIR CHRISTOPHER WREN
BRUCE ANGRAVE
1964
40 × 25 in/101.6 × 63.5 cm

121

ANCIENT AND MODERN mingle in London's countryside; new communities
have been grafted with understanding on to market towns that have
known the quiet of centuries. London Transport's new Country Walks book
links old with new, and the bustle of urban everyday with country peace.

Buy Country Walks (Book Two) 1967 edition at Underground station ticket offices, London Transport
Enquiry Offices, or post free from the Publicity Officer, Griffith House, 280, Marylebone Road, N.W.1.
Also obtainable at station bookstalls and branches of W. H. Smith Ltd.

ANCIENT AND MODERN
BILL LEESON
1967
40 × 25 in/101.6 × 63.5 cm

THE NEW TOWNS created in the 1950s and '60s in the countryside around London were a source of new traffic for London Transport's Green Line and country bus services.

SPRING in the air, *Country Walks* in your pocket, and over 200 miles of London's countryside at your feet. With notes and maps the current volume intimately describes 20 walks of varying lengths. Price 5/- from any London Transport Enquiry Office, at most Underground stations or post free from the Publicity Officer, Griffith House, 280 Marylebone Rd., N.W.1

EPPING FOREST turns the Cockney into a countryman. On East London's very doorstep lie nearly 6,000 acres of unspoiled countryside. Under its ancient trees, amid bracken and bramble, live the myriad flowers and animals of the Forest. You can roam at will for miles, you can have tea at High Beach, and on Connaught Water you can hire a boat and risk dress and dignity to demonstrate your seamanship. In Epping Forest, every day is Zoo Day.

The Underground is the quickest way to the Forest, via Loughton or Theydon Bois, and Green Line coaches 718 and 720 go through it on their way to Harlow, Epping, and Bishop's Stortford. Ask for the free book 'A Day in Epping Forest' at London Transport's main Travel Enquiry Offices—or write to the Public Relations Officer, London Transport, 55 Broadway, S.W.1.

SPRING
HARRY STEVENS
1963
40 × 25 in/101.6 × 63.5 cm

EPPING FOREST
R. F. MICKLEWRIGHT
1968
40 × 25 in/101.6 × 63.5 cm

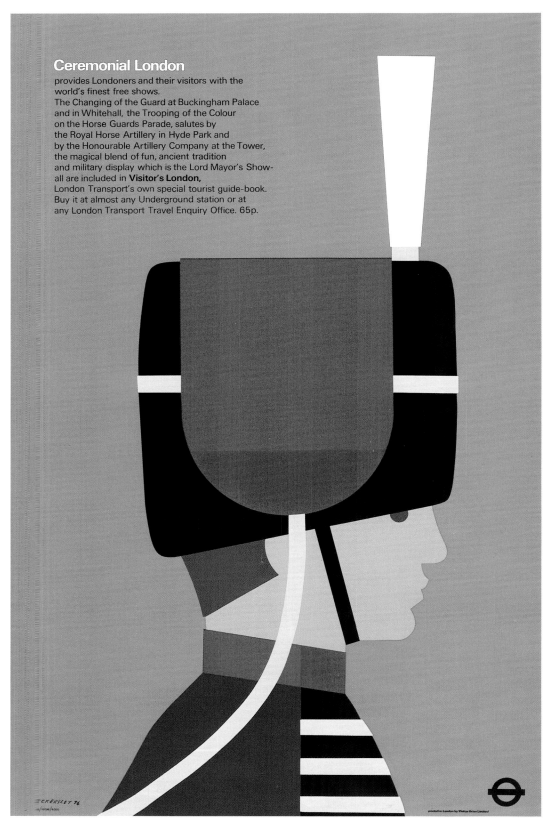

Ceremonial London

provides Londoners and their visitors with the
world's finest free shows.
The Changing of the Guard at Buckingham Palace
and in Whitehall, the Trooping of the Colour
on the Horse Guards Parade, salutes by
the Royal Horse Artillery in Hyde Park and
by the Honourable Artillery Company at the Tower,
the magical blend of fun, ancient tradition
and military display which is the Lord Mayor's Show-
all are included in **Visitor's London,**
London Transport's own special tourist guide-book.
Buy it at almost any Underground station or at
any London Transport Travel Enquiry Office. 65p.

CEREMONIAL LONDON
TOM ECKERSLEY
1976
40 × 25 in/101.6 × 63.5 cm

LIKE HIS CONTEMPORARY Abram Games,
Tom Eckersley has been designing
posters for London Transport since
the 1930s, but his later work in the
1960s and '70s is as strong as the early
designs he produced in partnership
with Eric Lombers before the war (see
page 92). He began making
extensive use of coloured paper
cut-outs for his artworks as a wider
range of colours became available in
the 1970s. In 1985, Eckersley became
the first artist to celebrate fifty years of
design work for London Transport
with a one-man retrospective
exhibition at the London Transport
Museum, for which he designed a new
Underground poster.

⊞ **London Transport Collection**

The London Transport collection of historic
vehicles: buses, trams trolleybuses, locomotives,
rolling stock, posters, signs, tickets
and other exhibits at Syon Park, Brentford.
Open every day except Christmas Day
and Boxing Day.
April to September 1000–1900,
October to March 1000–1700
or dusk (whichever is earlier),
admission 25p children 15p
(last tickets issued one hour before closing).
Underground to Hammersmith then
bus 267, or to Gunnersbury then bus 117
or 267. On Sundays buses E1 and E2
run beyond Brentford to Syon Park.
Green Line coach 701. British Rail
to Gunnersbury or Kew Bridge, then
buses 117 or 267; or to Syon Lane
then short walk.

CUT TRAVEL

LING TIME

Victoria line

a free leaflet includes an Underground map with details
of Victoria Line times, fares and how to use the automatic
gates. Ask at any of the London Transport Travel Offices
or write to the Public Relations Officer 55 Broadway SW1.
Phone Travel Enquiries 01-222 1234, any time, day or night

VICTORIA LINE
TOM ECKERSLEY
1969
40 × 25 in/101.5 × 63.5 cm

LONDON TRANSPORT COLLECTION
TOM ECKERSLEY
1975
40 × 25 in/101.6 × 63.5 cm

That'll be the day.

Fly the Tube

Take the Piccadilly Line to Heathrow Airport.
It's the only way to fly.

THAT'LL BE THE DAY
KIM WHEATER (FCB ADVERTISING)
1984
60 × 40 in/152.4 × 101.6 cm

ONE OF THE FIRST of a new series of large, four-sheet posters, introduced as space-fillers in the early 1980s, referred to the recently introduced practice of wheel-clamping illegally parked vehicles in central London. The absurd image of a clamped tube train makes the advantage of Underground travel immediately obvious.

FLY THE TUBE
GEOFF SENIOR (FCB ADVERTISING)
1977
40 × 25 in/101.6 × 63.5 cm

THE PICCADILLY LINE was extended from West London to Heathrow Airport in 1976. 'Fly the Tube', with its catchy title and clever composite photographs linking airliners and tube trains, was an award-winning poster designed by London Transport's advertising agency FCB, under the art direction of Brian Watson.

BUSABOUT
**HANS UNGER AND
EBERHARD SCHULZE**
1970
40 × 25 in/101.6 × 63.5 cm

UNGER worked with the mosaicist Eberhard Schulze on a number of architectural decoration schemes, and the pair of them used the same technique to produce poster artworks for London Transport. A proposal to incorporate the original mosaics into new station designs did not come to fruition.

BUSABOUT The London red bus, its top deck high above the traffic, is your ideal grandstand view-point, for historic buildings, places of interest and the endlessly entertaining hubbub of the teeming streets. A Red Bus Rover ticket gives you a day's travel-as-you-please on 1,500 miles of red bus routes and costs 7/- (child 3/6). A leaflet gives details. Another leaflet 'London from a Bus Top' suggests a lot of ways to use it. Ask at any London Transport Travel Enquiry office or write to the Public Relations Officer, 55 Broadway, S.W.1.

BY LONDON TRANSPORT ⊖

Printed in England by Sir Joseph Causton and Sons Ltd., London and Eastleigh

127

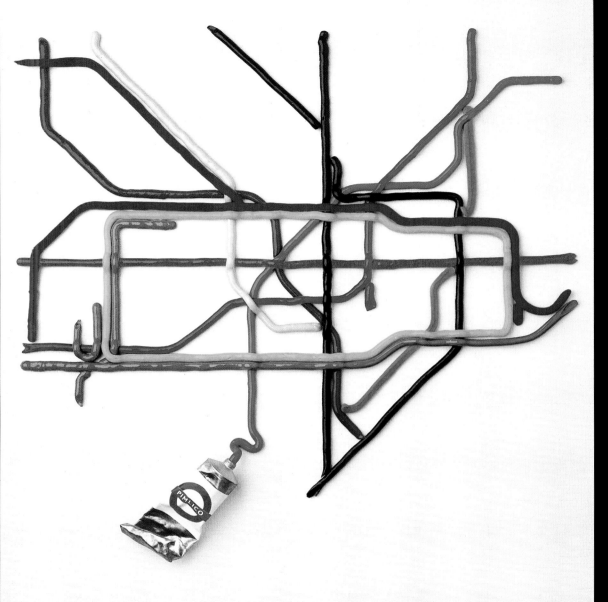

THE TATE GALLERY
by Tube

One of a series of new paintings commissioned by London Underground

Printed by Print Processes Ltd., London

THE TATE GALLERY
DAVID BOOTH
(THE FINE WHITE LINE
DESIGN)
1987
30 × 20 in/76.2 × 50.8 cm

THIS WAS one of the first, and most effective, of the new artworks commissioned by London Underground Ltd in the mid-1980s.

8

In 1984 London Transport was restructured to become a co-ordinating body with two subsidiary operating companies, London Buses Limited and London Underground Limited. All three businesses had to rethink their marketing and publicity strategies in a new climate of competition with a growing number of public services

being privatised or 'outsourced', reversing the trend of the 1930s. While LBL was gradually fragmented by the new route tendering process, LUL looked to reinforce its corporate identity with a strong emphasis on high design standards for the company. The policy of direct commissions to artists was revived, initially as a programme of corporate fine art sponsorship which was refined in the 1990s for inclusion within a broader advertising, publicity and marketing strategy. Transport *for* London, the successor body to London Transport established in 2000, plans to maintain and develop the revitalised artistic design standards of its predecessor in the new century.

Whitechapel Art Gallery
Next door to Aldgate East Station

WHITECHAPEL ART GALLERY
BRUCE MCLEAN
1989
60 × 40 in/152.4 × 101.6 cm

SIR JOHN SOANE'S MUSEUM
DAN FERN
1987
30 × 20 in/76.2 × 50.8 cm

A POSTER inspired by one of London's most unusual museums. Sir John Soane (1753–1837) was a leading Georgian architect who designed new buildings for the Bank of England in the 1790s The museum is in the house he designed for himself in 1812.

The Royal Academy of Arts
Nearest stations: Green Park, Piccadilly Circus

Royal Academy by Julian Trevelyan RA
Commissioned by the Royal Academy and London Underground

THE ROYAL ACADEMY OF ARTS
JULIAN TREVELYAN
1988
60 × 40 in/152.4 × 101.6 cm

A NUMBER of the well established artists commissioned for the 'Art on the Underground' programme were approached through the Royal Academy. This striking piece by Julian Trevelyan was one of the artist's last completed paintings.

The flamingoes by Tube

Golders Hill Park. Nearest stations: Golders Green, Hampstead

Days on the water

Nearest stations:
Hyde Park Corner, for the Serpentine
Baker Street, for Regent's Park Lake
Richmond, for the riverside

THE FLAMINGOES BY TUBE
KAY GALLWEY
1987
60 × 40 in/152.4 × 101.6 cm

DAYS ON THE WATER
SANDRA FISHER
1989
60 × 40 in/152.4 × 101.6 cm

The 'ART on the Underground' programme started in 1986 was not intended to produce publicity posters. These were commissioned works of art reproduced as posters, and were to be appreciated as such rather than to generate more customers for an already overloaded system. The use of possible destinations as subjects gave the scheme an overall consistency.

The new Kew by Tube

The Princess of Wales Conservatory. Nearest station Kew Gardens

THE NEW KEW BY TUBE
JENNIE TUFFS
1987
60 × 40 in/152.4 × 101.6 cm

133

JUST BECAUSE YOU'VE FINISHED WORK IT DOESN'T MEAN CURTAINS FOR YOUR TRAVELCARD. ⊖

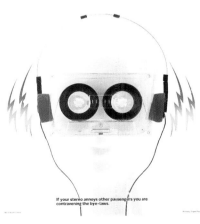

CURTAINS FOR YOUR TRAVELCARD
TREVOR CALEY
(FCB ADVERTISING)
1986
11⅘ × 23½ in/30 × 59.7 cm

THREE MOSAIC designs were used in 1986 to advertise Travelcards. They were reproduced both as 'car cards' for display inside trains and as giant 32-sheet posters to be viewed from station platforms across the track.

OR TAKE THE TUBE
NICK HARDCASTLE
(FCB ADVERTISING)
1987
40 × 25 in/101.6 × 63.5 cm

THIS AWARD-WINNING design made a disappointingly brief appearance on the Underground system.

KEEP YOUR PERSONAL STEREO *PERSONAL*!
TIM DEMUTH
1987
16¾ × 10¾ in/42.5 × 27.3 cm

PRODUCED for display inside Underground cars in response to complaints from passengers, this poster was so popular that, within a few weeks of its appearance, most copies had been stolen by the Underground's customers.

EXPLORE LONDON
CATHERINE DENVIR
1986
60 × 40 in/152.4 × 101.6 cm

Chinatown
by Underground

nearest station Leicester Square

Chinatown
John Bellany ARA

one of a series commissioned
by London Underground

Copyright London Underground Limited

CHINATOWN
JOHN BELLANY
1988
60 × 40 in/152.4 × 101.6 cm

JOHN BELLANY'S 'Chinatown' was the
most controversial new work
commissioned in the late 1980s, and
provoked quite a debate in the
London evening papers It is a
challenging and enigmatic picture
which breaks all the rules of poster
design by having no clear message
and remaining both mysterious and
a little disturbing to the viewer.

The Museum of Mankind, by Tube

Burlington Gardens W1
Nearest stations: Green Park & Piccadilly Circus

Diviner Mask and Lizard by Tom Wood
A new work of art commissioned by London Underground

London Underground Limited

MUSEUM OF MANKIND
TOM WOOD
1989
60 × 40 in/152.4 × 101.6 cm

THIS DRAMATIC poster reproduced one of a series of pictures based on the idea of a 'Diviner' who 'casts' objects in order to foretell the future. The various elements were all inspired by objects in the Museum of Mankind, the ethnographic branch of the British Museum whose collections have since been moved back to the main museum in Bloomsbury.

WEEDONHILL WOOD
LUCAS KUYS
1992
60 × 40 in/152.4 × 101.6 cm

THIS PAINTING was commissioned in 1992 to mark the centenary of the Metropolitan's arrival in rural Buckinghamshire. Amersham is stil a small country town today despite its hundred year link with the London Underground. Dutch artist Lucas Kuys felt that his biggest challenge as an 'outsider' was how to sum up the collective British idea of the countryside in one work of art. The London Underground press release described the result as 'a highly personalised, *definitely* unBritish view of the Bucks landscape that combines a robust, masterly technique with idiosyncratic references to landscape forms and their juxtaposition in space.'

HIGHGATE PONDS
HOWARD HODGKIN
1989
60 × 40 in/152.4 × 101.6 cm

THE FIRST of the 'Art on the Underground' commissions tc be bled to the borders when reproduced as a poster.

LONDON'S PARKS
JENNIE TUFFS
1997
60 × 40 in/152.4 × 101.6 cm

London's parks
by bus and tube

A new work commissioned for London Transport Art
Artist, Jannie Tuffs

London Transport

Posters available at London Transport Museum, Covent Garden

Supported by
TDI

Find Michelangelo at the V&A

Nearest station South Kensington

Find Michelangelo at the V&A by R B Kitaj RA
A new work of art commissioned by London Underground ©

FIND MICHELANGELO AT THE V&A
R B KITAJ
1993
60 x 40 in/152.4 x 101.6 cm

MONUMENT
JEFFERY CAMP
1991
60 x 40 in/152.4 x 101.6 cm

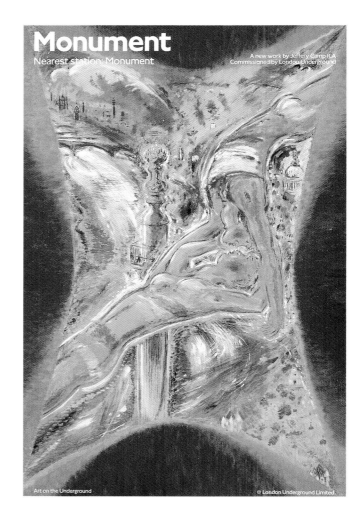

London's new architecture by bus and tube

A new work commissioned for London Transport Art
Artist, Edwina Ellis

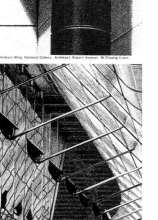  

© London Transport

Posters and postcards available at London Transport Museum, Covent Garden

Supported by

LONDON'S NEW ARCHITECTURE
EDWINA ELLIS
1996
40 x 25 in/101.6 x 63.5 cm

NINE ARTWORKS in one poster celebrating the diversity of modern architecture in London. This was one of the first posters to be sponsored by TDI, who won the tender to manage and run the commercial advertising for London Underground.

DANCING IN THE STREET
PAULA COX
1994
60 × 40 in/152.4 × 101.6 cm

ALTHOUGH NOT promoting a particular event, this was posted in the run up to the Notting Hill Carnival, London's annual street festival and celebration of Afro-Caribbean culture, which takes place over the August Bank Holiday.

THINK WHAT YOU SAVE
BAINSFAIR SHARKEY TROTT AGENCY
1992
12⁴/₅ × 23¹/₄ in/30 × 59.2 cm

USING ART to encourage responsible behaviour by passengers, 'Think what you save' was part of a campaign to counter fare evasion. Munch's picture 'The Scream', to which the poster makes a visual reference, is an interesting example of a once obscure work of art which in recent years has become a widely recognised image of alienation.

Please take your litter home

You may have noticed that for the time being all litter bins have been removed from the Underground. Now more than ever we need your help to keep the trains and stations tidy and safe.

Please take all your litter home with you.

PLEASE TAKE YOUR LITTER HOME
RICHARD SPICE
1991
40 x 25 in/101.6 x 63.5 cm

REMOVING LITTER bins from the Underground was one of the safety measures taken after the enquiry into the King's Cross fire disaster in 1937.

shopping

Get on board ⊖ London's Buses.

SHOPPING
ALAN FLETCHER
1986
40 x 25 in/101.6 x 63.5 cm

WE WANT TO MAKE YOUR JOURNEY EASIER
BMP (BOSE MASSIMI POLLITT) AGENCY
2000
$11^4/5$ x $23^3/4$ in/30.3 x 60.5 cm

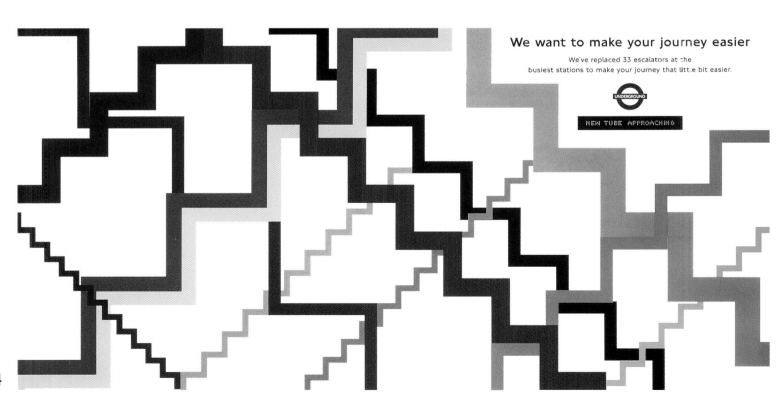

We want to make your journey easier

We've replaced 33 escalators at the
busiest stations to make your journey that little bit easier.

⊖ UNDERGROUND

NEW TUBE APPROACHING

100 years of Underground Electric Railways
AN EXHIBITION AT THE LONDON TRANSPORT MUSEUM, COVENT GARDEN

TUBE CENTENARY
SUE TURNER (THE FINE WHITE LINE DESIGN)
1990
30 × 20 in/76.2 × 50.8 cm

WE WANT TO MAKE YOUR JOURNEY SMOOTHER
BMP (BOSE MASSIMI POLLITT) AGENCY
2000
11⁴/₅ × 23³/₄ in/30.3 × 60.5 cm

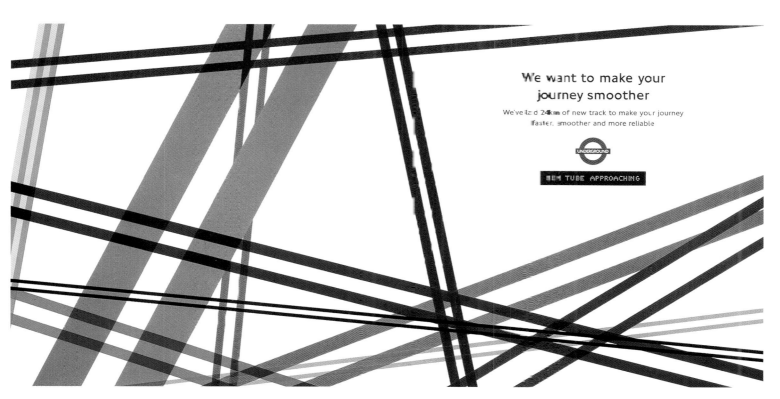

We want to make your
journey smoother

We've laid 24km of new track to make your journey
faster, smoother and more reliable

UNDERGROUND

TUBE APPROACHING

CREATIVE USES of photography in examples from publicity campaigns on fare dodging and safety

WE DELIVERED THE MIDWIFE
BAINSFAIR SHARKEY TROTT AGENCY
1996
40 x 25 in/101.6 x 63.5 cm

RUSHING
BMP (BOSE MASSIMI POLLITT) AGENCY
1998
22¹/₂ x 15³/₄ in/57.2 x 40.4 cm

SIXTY YEARS PASSENGER SERVICE FOR THE CAPITAL

SIXTY YEARS
PASSENGER SERVICE
FOR THE CAPITAL
TRICKETT & WEBB
1993
40 × 25 in./101.6 ×
63.5 cm

A POPULAR POSTER
commissioned to
celebrate London
Transport's sixtieth
birthday in 1993, with
extensive use of the
familiar roundel
symbol in various
guises and Johnston's
classic Underground
lettering.

The 'SIMPLY' series was a long running publicity campaign using a wide range of artwork styles unified by the strapline and linked to different themes. These appeared as both posters and covers to leaflets detailing venues for leisure activities from night clubs to restaurants, and how to get there by bus or Tube.

SIMPLY SPRING
REG CARTWRIGHT
1998
40 × 25 in/
101.6 × 63.5 cm

Simply Spring by Tube and bus

Painting commissioned by London Transport from Reg Cartwright.

This poster is available from
the London Transport Museum, Covent Garden Piazza.

Supported by
TDI

148

Simply Nightlife by Tube and bus

Collage commissioned by London Transport from Dan Fern.
This poster is available from the London Transport Museum, Covent Garden Piazza.

Supported by

TDI

Simply Music by Tube and bus

Computer generated digital art commissioned by London Transport from Paul Wearing.
This poster is available from the London Transport Museum, Covent Garden Piazza.

Simply Appetising by Tube and bus

'A Little Of What You Fancy' commissioned by London Transport from Michael Forbes.
This poster is available from the London Transport Museum, Covent Garden Piazza.

SIMPLY MUSIC
PAUL WEARING
1999
40 × 25 in/101.6 × 63.5 cm

SIMPLY APPETISING
MICHAEL FORBES
2000
40 × 25 in/101.6 × 63.5 cm

149

Eros And Home
**BMP (Bose Massimi
Pollitt) agency**
Photographer/
Illustrator: Giles
Revell
1997
60 × 40 in/152.4 ×
101.6 cm

Making London simple

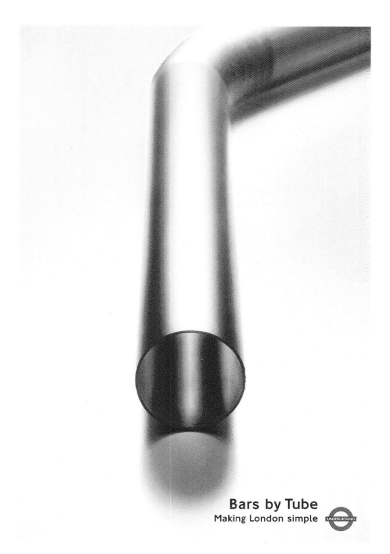

BARS BY TUBE
BMP (BOSE MASSIMI POLLITT) AGENCY
PHOTOGRAPHY BY DAVID GILL
2000
18 × 11⁴/₅ in/45.2 × 30 cm

GARDENS BY TUBE
BMP (BOSE MASSIMI POLLITT) AGENCY
PHOTOGRAPHY BY DAVID GILL
2000
8 × 11⁴/₅ in/45.2 × 30 cm

Bars by Tube
Making London simple

'MAKING LONDON SIMPLE' was another strapline
for a themed publicity campaign that produced
some effective creative images from agency BMP.

Gardens by Tube
Making London simple

The view of the House, by Tube

Nearest stations: Vauxhall and Waterloo

Westminster Palace from Lambeth Bridge by Frederick Gore CBE, RA
A new work of art commissioned by London Underground

Art on the Underground

© London Underground Limited

THE VIEW OF THE HOUSE
FREDERICK GORE
1991
60 × 40 in/152.4 × 101.6 cm

TATE GALLERY
DAVID HOCKNEY
1997
40 × 25 in/101.6 × 63.5 cm

THREE ARTISTS' views of London landmarks new and old. Frederick Gore depicts the Houses of Parliament from Lambeth Bridge. David Hockney's work celebrated the centenary of the Tate Gallery on Millbank. John Miller's view of the river, the last art poster produced by London Transport before Transport *for* London took over, appropriately features Tate Modern, London's magnificent new gallery of modern art. Tate Modern is housed in the former Bankside power station and was one of the biggest Millennium projects in the city.

Tate Gallery
by bus and tube

Nearest tube: Pimlico
Buses: 2, 36, 77A, 88, 185

A new work commissioned for London Transport Art
Artist: David Hockney

Celebration, 1997, oil on canvas, 21¼ x 13¼", © David Hockney
Posters available at London Transport Museum & Tate Gallery

Supported by

152

SIMPLY RIVER
JOHN MILLER
2000
60 × 40 in/152.4 ×
101.6 cm

Simply River by Tube and bus

Painting commissioned by London Transport from John Miller.

This poster is available from the London Transport Museum, Covent Garden Piazza.

153

Notes on Artists

The author and publishers have made every effort to discover details about all the artists whose work is represented in this book, but regret that in some cases no information has been forthcoming.

SYBIL ANDREWS 1898–1992
Born in Bury St Edmunds, her first art training was on JOHN HASSALL'S Correspondence Course in 1918. She later attended Heatherley's School of Fine Art and the New Grosvenor School of Modern Art in London. At the Grosvenor she met Claude Flight who taught lino-cutting, and this became her favourite medium. She shared a studio with Cyril Power, another member of Flight's circle; all of them worked in an avant-garde, Futurist style. Her posters for London Transport, were given the joint signature 'Andrew Power'. She moved to Hampshire in the late 1930s and emigrated to British Columbia, Canada, after the war.
6 posters, 1 panel poster, 1933–35. Page 94

BRUCE ANGRAVE d. 1983
Born in Leicester, he studied at Chiswick Art School, Ealing School of Art and the Central School of Art, London. He worked as a freelance book and periodical illustrator, designer and sculptor (including paper works for the Festival of Britain in 1951 and Expo 70 in Japan). His poster designs were influenced by TOM ECKERSLEY, Lewitt-Him and ABRAM GAMES.
8 posters, 1942–64. Page 121

MAXWELL ASHBY ARMFIELD, RWS 1881–1972
Born in Ringwood, Hampshire, he studied at the Birmingham School of Art under Arthur Gaskin, in Paris and in Italy, and lived in the USA from 1915 to 1922. A Theosophist, he was co-director of the Greenleaf Theatre Drama School and lectured on stage design while also working as a painter, etcher, illustrator, poet and writer. His tempera works were influenced by early Dutch and Italian Quattrocento painting. A retrospective exhibition of his work was held at the Southampton Art Gallery in 1978.
2 posters, 1915. Page 34

CHARLES GERARD ATKINSON b. 1879
Born in Seaford, Sussex, he studied art in Liverpool and in the studio of Walter Hilton, then worked as a painter.
2 posters, 1933. Page 87

MABEL LUCIE ATTWELL 1879–1964
Born in the East End of London, the ninth of a butcher's ten children, she studied at the Regent Street Art School and at Heatherley's, but completed neither course. Starting out as an illustrator of children's books, she was equally successful as a postcard designer for Valentine's of Dundee, for whom she produced work from 1911 until the end of her life. A contributor to annuals and gift books, she published Lucie Attwell's Children's Annual from 1922 to 1957. She also designed advertisements. posters, calendars, figurines and wall plaques.
3 posters, 1913. Page 20

ROBERT SARGENT AUSTIN, RA 1895–1973
Born in Leicester, he attended Leicester School of Art and in 1911 became apprenticed as a printer and lithographer. He received a scholarship to the Royal College of Art, where he studied engraving under Frank Short 1914–16 and 1919–22; this was followed by a year at the British School in Rome (where he was elected to the faculty in 1926). He taught engraving at the Royal College of Art 1927–44 and was Professor of Graphic Design 1948–55. A successful etcher and engraver, he also produced pencil illustrations for several travel books on which he collaborated with his wife, Ada Harrison.
Series of 4 posters, 1943. Page 105

JOHN BAINBRIDGE 1918–78
Born in Sydney, Australia, he was educated in Melbourne at the Swinbourne Art School and the National Gallery School. In 1940 he was appointed art director of the National Theatre, Melbourne, and exhibited throughout Australia. He moved to England in 1945, where he worked as an exhibition designer, poster artist, documentary film maker, and designer of theatre sets and costumes. In 1959 he was elected a Fellow of the Society of Industrial Artists.
5 posters, 1 panel poster, 1953–7. Pages 106, 107

DORA BATTY d. 1966
The most prolific of the women artists who worked for the Underground, in the 1920s she also produced designs for the Poole Pottery, notably their farmyard series for children, and publicity work for MacFisheries. From 1932 to 1958 she was a tutor in the Textiles Department at the Central School of Arts and Crafts, London.
27 posters, 18 panel posters, 1921–38. Pages 73, 78

EDWARD BAWDEN, RA, RDI 1903–89
Born in Braintree, Essex, he studied at the Cambridge School of Art (1919–22) and the Royal College of Art, London (1922–5), where PAUL NASH was a tutor and major influence. He collaborated with his friends ERIC RAVILIOUS and Cyril Mahoney on mural designs for Morley College (1928–30). Bawden became a successful and prolific illustrator and graphic designer, working freelance for a wide variety of organizations on posters, advertisements, book illustrations, ceramic decorations, wallpaper and textile designs. He taught graphic design at the Royal College of Art 1930–40 and 1948–53, and was made a Royal Designer for Industry in 1948. A major exhibition of his work was held at the Fine Art Society, London, in 1987.
11 posters, 4 panel posters, 1924–52. Pages 14, 83, 108

JOHN BELLANY, RA b. 1942
Born in Port Seton, Scotland, the son and grandson of fishermen, he studied at the Edinburgh College of Art (1960–5) and the Royal College of Art (1965–8) under Carel Weight and Peter de Francia. He has taught painting at various colleges of art, and was Head of the Faculty of Painting at Croydon College 1973–8. A major retrospective exhibition of his work was held in 1986 by

the Scottish National Gallery of Modern Art, Edinburgh, later shown at the Serpentine Gallery, London.
2 posters, 1988–90. Page 136

L. B. BLACK
4 posters, 1926–7. Page 63

DAVID BOOTH
Commissioned via The Fine White Line Design agency.
1 poster, 1987. Page 128

FRANK WILLIAM BRANGWYN, RA, RWS 1867–1956
Born in Bruges, Belgium, he moved to London with his family in 1875. He studied at the South Kensington School of Art, worked in the William Morris shop in Oxford Street from 1882 to 1884, and exhibited at the Royal Academy from 1885. He spent even years as a sailor from 1887. On his return, he worked as a painter, designer and craftsman in many media and by 1913 had achieved a considerable reputation, with projects such as interiors for the British pavilions at the Venice Biennales of 1905 and 1907. He illustrated numerous books, designed the stained glass for St Patrick's Cathedral, Dublin, in 1931, and exhibited widely in Britain and on the Continent. There is a Brangwyn Museum in Bruges.
3 posters, 1913–17. Pages 22, 30

PERCY DRAKE BROOKSHAW 1907–93
Born in Southwark, London, he became a painter in oils and watercolour as well as a lithographer. Encouraged by GREGORY BROWN, he produced illustrations and advertising material as well as posters. He taught lithography at Goldsmiths College of Art and was a member of the Art Workers' Guild and the Senefelder Club.
4 posters, 5 panel posters, 1928–58. Page 51

F. GREGORY BROWN 1887–1948
After an apprenticeship with an art metalworker in 1903, he turned to illustration, with his first important commissions from magazines. A founder-member of the Design and Industries Association in 1915, he became a poster designer, working for ICI, MacFisheries and the mainline railway companies, as well as for the Underground. From 1920 onwards, he also designed textiles for which he won a gold medal at the 1925 Paris Exhibition of Decorative Arts.
48 posters; 13 panel posters, 1916–40. Pages 37, 45

DOROTHY MARY BURROUGHES d. 1963
She studied art at the Slade School, Heatherley's School of Fine Art and in Germany, before becoming a poster designer and illustrator of books and magazines, specializing in natural history subjects.
2 posters, 1920–2. Page 66

CHARLES BURTON b. 1882
Born in Chesterfield, Derbyshire, he studied art in London, France and Belgium. He later worked as a commercial and industrial artist for shipping companies,

railways and other national advertisers.
6 posters, 16 panel posters, 1930. Pages 51, 75

TREVOR CALEY b. 1943
Born in London, he attended the Chelsea School of Art, specializing in mural design. He works in a range of media from stained glass to concrete relief; in 1984–5, he worked with Eduardo Paolozzi on the mosaics at Tottenham Court Road Underground station.
3 posters, 1986. Page 134

JEFFERY CAMP, RA b. 1923
Trained at Edinburgh College of Art, he is noted as a painter of figures and landscapes in oils. His first solo exhibition was in 1959, and he has exhibited extensively since then in London and abroad. In 1961 he was elected a member of the London Group, and from 1963–74 he taught at the Slade School of Art.
1 poster, 1991. Page 140

REG CARTWRIGHT b. 1939
Born in Leicester, he worked as a commercial artist for thirteen years after doing national service. In 1974 he took up painting and illustration full time.
1 poster, 1998. Page 148

GAYNOR CHAPMAN b. 1935
Born in London, she studied at the Royal College of Art in 1955–8, and works mainly as a book illustrator and tutor in graphic design.
6 posters, 1962–76. Page 115

GEORGE CLAUSEN, RA 1852–1944
Born in London, the son of a decorative painter, he joined his father's firm at sixteen to become a furniture designer and took evening classes at the South Kensington School of Art. Encouraged by his tutor Edwin Long he won a scholarship for full-time study at the school (1873–5), then worked as Long's assistant. A painter of rustic scenes, decorative artist and engraver, he also designed posters in the 1920s for the London Midland & Scottish Railway.
1 poster, 1917. Page 38

AUSTIN COOPER 1890–1964
Born on the prairie in Manitoba, Canada, he was sent to Europe as a child and studied at the Cardiff School of Art from the age of thirteen, before winning a scholarship to the Allan-Frazer Art College, Arbroath (1906–10). He returned to Canada and began a career as a commercial artist in Montreal. Settling in London in 1922, he received the first of many poster commissions from London Underground. The first Principal of the Reimann School of Commercial and Industrial Art (1936–40), he turned from his career as a poster artist in 1943 to become a full-time painter.
54 posters, 1922–44. Page 63

ALDO COSOMATI
Born in Italy, he settled in London in about 1920 after training at German and Swiss art schools. This included five years in Zurich where he studied drawing, printing, bookbinding, and furniture design. He specialized in commercial art.
13 posters, 9 panel posters, 1923–8. Page 74

PAULA COX b. 1950
Studied at Camberwell College of Art and Brighton University. Her work has been exhibited extensively throughout Britain and in Barcelona. She has designed programmes, book and record covers as well as tapestries, carpets, t-shirts and murals.
1 poster, 1994. Page 42

VERNEY L. DANVERS
A poster artist who ran a school of commercial art and had commissions from fashion and interior design companies.
9 posters, 32 panel posters, 1922–5. Page 42

LEN DEIGHTON b. 1929
Born in London, he studied at St Martin's School of Art and the Royal College of Art. He worked as an illustrator in New York, then as art director for an advertising agency in London. The Ipcress File (1962) marked the beginning of his second career as a best-selling author.
1 poster, 1957. Page 114

TIM DEMUTH b. 1942
Born in Oxshott, Surrey, he went to Kingston School of Art (1959–62) to study graphic design. After several years as a designer/typographer he joined the London Transport Advertising and Publicity Office in 1971, becoming art director with London Buses and London Underground in the 1980s. He has worked on adaptations of the Underground map, timetables, signage, and other aspects of corporate identity.
15 posters, 15 panel posters, 1971–89. Page 134

CATHERINE DENVIR b. 1953
Born in Bethersden, Kent, she studied at the Chelsea School of Art. Her illustrations have appeared in magazines advertisements, posters and brochures for a wide range of commercial clients,
1 poster, 1986. Page 135

ERNEST MICHAEL DINKEL 1895–1983
Born in Huddersfield, Yorkshire, he studied at the local technical college, then at the Royal College of Art, London. He worked as a painter and designer, notably of inn signs.
4 posters, 1931–3. Page 52

DOROTHY DIX
Landscape painter.
1 poster, 1922. Page 45

JAMES H. DOWD 1884–1956
Draughtsman, etcher and painter who specialized in illustrations of children. From 1906 he contributed to Punch and became the magazine's first film cartoonist.
5 posters, 1924–6. Page 62

LILIAN M. DRING b. 1908
Born Lilian Welch in Surbiton, Surrey, she trained at Kingston School of Art and the Royal College of Art. The career in poster design she had hoped for was frustrated by the Depression years and she became a designer-embroiderer specializing in hand and machine stitched appliqué.
1 poster artwork, c. 1933. Page 78

JEAN DUPAS 1882–1964
Born in Bordeaux, France, he studied at the Ecole des Beaux Arts in Paris. He won a gold medal at the Salon des Artistes Français in 1922; as a result his decorative panels and poster designs became highly fashionable. He had a number of prestigious commercial clients in France, England and the USA, including the Sèvres Factory and Saks Department store in New York.
5 posters, 1930–3. Page 79

ANTHONY ECKERSLEY b. 1937
The son of TOM ECKERSLEY, he received his design education at the London College of Printing, and worked on editorial design for Vogue magazine before going into advertising.
1 poster, 1964. Page 121

TOM ECKERSLEY, RDI 1914–97
Born in Lowton, Lancashire, he studied at the Salford School of Art (1930–4), and then worked in London in partnership with his college friend Eric Lombers (1914–78). In 1935, their former tutor recommended them to Frank Pick: their design for a small Underground car panel poster marked the beginning of a long and productive working relationship. Largely specializing in poster design, Eckersley Lombers soon counted many important companies among their clients including Shell, the General Post Office and the BBC. The partnership was brought to an end by the outbreak of the war. Eckersley worked as a cartographer in the RAF and produced a series of 'war effort' posters. He was head of the Graphic Design Department at the London College of Printing from 1953 to 1977, and was made a Royal Designer for Industry in 1963.
13 posters, 15 panel posters with Eric Lombers; 22 posters, 14 panel posters alone, 1935–95. Pages 92, 95, 124–25

CLIFFORD and ROSEMARY ELLIS 1907–85 and 1910–98
Married in 1931, they collaborated on poster designs for Shell, the Empire Marketing Board and the General Post Office as well as for London Transport. Between 1945 and 1982, they designed nearly one hundred book jackets for the New Naturalist series published by Collins.
12 posters, 9 panel posters, 1933–7. Pages 80, 81, 95

EDWINA ELLIS b. 1946
Born in Sydney, Australia, she studied printing at the National Art School (1963–69). In 1972 she moved to London and studied metal engraving at John Cass College 1972–73 and wood engraving at Simon Brett Summer School in 1981 and 1983. In 1985 she was elected a fellow of the Royal Society of Painter Printmakers.
1 poster, 1996. Page 141

ALMA FAULKNER
4 posters, 1925–8. Pages 53, 59

DEN FERN b. 1945
Studied graphic design at the Manchester College of Art and Design (1963–7) then illustration at the Royal College of Art, London (1967–70). He worked in Amsterdam 1970–3, then settled as a freelance

illustrator in London, working for a wide range of clients including magazine and book publishers, design consultancies, record and theatre companies and advertising agencies. Appointed Head of Illustration at the Royal College of Art in 1986, he became the department's first Professor in 1989.
2 posters, 1987–8, Page 130, 149

SANDRA FISHER 1947–94
Born in New York City, she studied at the Chouinard Art School, California Institute of the Arts, Los Angeles, and moved to London in 1971. She was guest lecturer and visiting artist at various art schools, including the Ruskin School of Drawing, Oxford, and the Byam Shaw School in London from 1976. She exhibited widely, principally in Britain, and had solo exhibitions in London in 1982 and 1987. Married R.B. KITAJ in 1983.
2 posters, 1989. Page 132

JAMES FITTON, RA 1899–1982
Born in Oldham, Lancashire, he trained as a fabric designer, then went to Manchester School of Art, financing his studies with nightshift work in the docks. He moved to London in 1923, where he studied and later taught lithography at the Central School of Art and Design. A successful freelance commercial artist, he worked in advertising and on book illustrations; he was a founder-member of the Artists International Association in 1933.
14 posters, 1932–43. Page 86

ALAN FLETCHER b. 1931
Born in Nairobi, Kenya, but brought up in England from the age of five. He studied art first at Hammersmith, then at the Central School and finally the Royal College of Art under F.H.K. Henrion and Herbert Spencer before gaining a scholarship to Yale University. He became a successful designer in the USA before founding Fletcher, Forbes, Gill in 1962, soon a leading graphic design group. In 1972 he co-founded the Pentagram design group. He created his own company in 1992 and was Designer of the Year in 1993.
2 posters, 1986. Page 144

FLETCHER
1 poster, 1926. Page 68

MICHAEL FORBES b. 1968
Born in Dingwall, Scotland, he took up painting full time in 1989 and is entirely self taught. George Melly has described his surreal images as 'truly impressive', paintings that are 'windows opening to an inner landscape'.
1 poster, 2000. Page 149

FOUGASSE 1887–1965
Born Cyril Kenneth Bird in London, the son of England cricketer Arthur Bird, he studied engineering at King's College, London, at his father's insistence, but attended evening art classes at the Regent Street Polytechnic and the London County Council School of Photo engraving and Lithography. Badly wounded in the First World War, he took lessons by correspondence from Percy Bradshaw's Press Art School. *Punch* started to publish his cartoons in 1916 under his pseudonym 'Fougasse' (a small land mine of unpredictable performance); this was to avoid confusion with another *Punch* artist, W. Bird. He

later became the magazine's Art Editor (1937), then its Editor (1949–53). During the Second World War he designed visual propaganda for nearly every government ministry as well as charities and voluntary groups; his famous 'Careless Talk Costs Lives' series was produced for the Ministry of Information.
13 posters, 7 panel posters, 1925–44. Pages 100, 101

ALFRED FRANCE
9 posters, 1910–12. Page 23

ERIC GEORGE FRASER 1902–83
Born in London, he attended W. R. Sickert's evening classes at Westminster School of Art and went on to Goldsmith's College (1919–24) where CLIVE GARDINER was his tutor. Fraser worked as an illustrator for *Radio Times* from 1926 and many other magazines, and designed posters for Shell, the General Post Office and the Ministry of Information. He produced murals for the British Empire Exhibitions in 1923 and 1938, and for the Origins of the People Pavilion at the Festival of Britain, 1951.
3 posters, 2 panel posters, 1925–8. Page 73

BARNETT FREEDMAN, RDI 1901–58
Born in Stepney, East London, the son of Russian Jews, he worked as a signwriter and a stonemason's and architect's assistant while attending evening classes at St Martin's School of Art (1916–22); he then studied painting at the Royal College of Art (1922–5). A pioneer in the revival of colour lithography, he illustrated numerous literary works as well as designing publicity material for Shell, the BBC and the General Post Office. In 1935, his work was included in the British Art in Industry exhibition at the Royal Academy; the same year his design was selected for the George V jubilee postage stamp. He was made a Royal Designer for Industry in 1949. On his death the Arts Council organized a memorial exhibition.
16 posters, 10 panel posters, 1936–7. Page 86

KAY GALLWEY b. 1936
Born in London, she studied at the City and Guilds and Goldsmith's Schools of Art (1951–3) and the Royal Academy (1953–7). A painter in oils and pastels, she has also designed costumes for theatre, television and films and fashion illustrations for magazines.
2 posters, 1987. Page 132

ABRAM GAMES, RDI 1914–96
Born in London, the son of an artist-photographer, he went to art school for only six months, then continued with evening classes while working for a commercial studio (1932–6). In 1935 he won the first prize in a London County Council poster competition; from 1936–40 he worked as a freelance poster artist. In 1941, he proposed to the War Office that designers be used on instructional and educational posters for the army; the scheme was so successful that he was appointed Official War Office Poster Designer, later assisted by Frank Newbould. After the war he specialized in designing posters and symbols: his work includes the Festival of Britain symbol (1951) and the BBC TV symbol (1953). He was a visiting lecturer in graphic design at the Royal College of Art (1946–53), and was made a Royal Designer for Industry in 1959.
18 posters, 1 panel poster, 1937–76. Pages 117, 118

ALFRED CLIVE GARDINER 1891–1960
Born in Blackburn, Lancashire, he attended the Slade School of Fine Art (1909–12) and the Royal Academy Schools (1913–14). He taught art at Goldsmith's College School of Art where he became Headmaster in 1929, then Principal in 1952. GRAHAM SUTHERLAND is among the pupils who have acknowledged his influence.
27 posters, 1926–51. Page 57

DAVID WILLIAM GENTLEMAN, RDI b. 1930
Born in London, he studied at St Albans School of Art (1947–8) and the Royal College of Art (1950–3) where he later taught (1953–5). Since then, he has worked as a freelance illustrator and designer, his commissions ranging from murals (including the Northern Line Charing Cross Underground station platforms in 1979) to postage stamps, carried out in a variety of media. He has done work for *The Observer* and *Sunday Times*, and was made a Royal Designer for Industry in 1970.
4 posters, 1956–7. Page 120

ROBERT JOHN GIBBINGS 1889–1958
Born in Cork, Ireland, where he briefly attended medical school. From 1912, he studied at the Slade School of Fine Art, then attended Noel Rooke's classes in wood engraving, a controversial part of the book illustration course at the Central School of Arts and Crafts. He founded the Society of Wood Engravers in 1919, then bought the Golden Cockerel Press in 1924, which he ran until 1933; of the 72 titles published, he decorated 19 with his own wood engravings and commissioned illustrations from a number of artists including Eric Gill, John Nash and ERIC RAVILIOUS.
1 poster, 1922. Page 56

FREDERICK GORE CBE, RA b. 1913
Son of the Camden Town Group painter Frederick Spencer Gore (1878–1914), he studied at Westminster School of Art and at the Slade. He held his first solo exhibition at the Redfern Gallery in 1937 and has exhibited at the Royal Academy since 1945. He is primarily a painter of urban scenes, figures and landscapes in oils. Gore has taught at Westminster and Chelsea Schools of Art and was the Head of Painting at St Martin's School of Art from 1959–79. From 1976–37 he was Chairman of the Royal Academy Exhibition Committee.
1 poster, 1991. Page 152

JOHN GRIFFITHS
1 poster, 1965. Page 120

AUBREY HAMMOND 1894–1940
Born in Folkestone, Kent, he studied at the Byam Shaw School of Art and at the Academie Julian in Paris. He later worked as a stage and poster designer and a caricaturist, and taught commercial and theatrical design at the Westminster School of Art..
7 posters, 1923–34. Page 70

NICK HARDCASTLE b. 1957
A freelance illustrator born in Norfolk, he studied at the Maidstone College of Art (1975–8) and the Royal College of Art (1978–81). In 1995 he designed a series of murals for the refurbished stations on the East London line.
1 poster, 1987. Page 134

ARCHIBALD STANDISH HARTRICK, RWS
1864–1950
Born in Bangalore, India, he went to Edinburgh University, then studied art at the Slade (1884–5) and the Academie Julian, Paris (1885–6); among his friends in France were Gauguin, Van Gogh and Toulouse Lautrec. Back in London, he worked as a magazine illustrator, and was on the staff of *The Graphic* (1890–3). From 1908, he taught at the Camberwell School of Art and, from 1914, at the Central School of Arts and Crafts. A book illustrator and watercolourist, he was a founder member of the Chelsea Arts Club.
3 posters, 1913–15; 1 set of lithographs, 1919. Pages 40–1

JOHN HASSALL 1868–1943
Born in Deal, Kent, he was educated in Devon and Heidelberg, Germany, followed by a stint of farming in Canada when he began contributing to *The Graphic*. Between 1891 and 1894 he studied in Antwerp, Belgium, then went to the Academie Julian in Paris. Back in England, he started illustrating children's books in the 1890s and became a successful advertising artist, cartoonist and poster designer with 'Skegness is So Bracing' (1908) for the Great Northern Railway one of his classics. An early member and later President of the London Sketch Club, he founded the New Art School (later the Hassall School of Art), which he ran for twenty years.
3 posters, 1908–13. Pages 20, 21

VICTOR HEMBROW
4 posters, 1926–8. Page 43

KEITH HENDERSON 1883–1982
Born in Scotland, he studied at the Slade School of Fine Art and in Paris where he shared a studio with MAXWELL ARMFIELD. Principally a painter and muralist who exhibited at leading London galleries and whose work is represented in many public collections, he also worked as an illustrator.
1 poster, 1935. Page 79

FREDERIC CHARLES HERRICK 1887–1970
He studied at Leicester College of Art and Crafts and the Royal College of Art. He designed the famous Wembley Lion logo for the British Empire Exhibition in 1924 and also worked as a painter. Most of his many Underground posters were designed for the Baynard Press, where he was Head of Studio.
42 posters, 1 panel poster, 1920–33. Pages 53, 61, 72

DAVID HOCKNEY, RA b. 1937
Born in Bradford, he studied at Bradford School of Art and at the Royal College of Art with R.B. KITAJ. During 1963–7 he settled in California and became the best internationally known British artist of his generation. He has worked in a wide variety of media including acrylics, etching, lithography, photography and even fax art. The first major exhibition of his work was held in 1970 at the Whitechapel Art Gallery and he has since exhibited world-wide.
1 poster, 1997. Page 152

HOWARD HODGKIN b. 1932
Born in London, he studied at Camberwell and then the Bath Academy of Art, later teaching at Charterhouse

School and then Corsham. His first exhibition was in 1962 but he only received critical attention in the 1970s. His painting has been described as 'a balance between figurative and abstract art, in the tradition of Matisse'. In 1981 his work was selected by the Royal Academy of Arts for an international touring exhibition and in 1985 he won the Turner Prize.
1 poster, 1989. Page 138

CHRISTINE H. JACKSON
Children's book illustrator.
6 posters, 19 press advertisements 1929–31. Page 47

MARGARET CALKIN JAMES 1895–1985
Trained at the Central School of Arts and Crafts, specializing in calligraphy and opened a workshop in Bloomsbury. She designed lampshades, stage props, posters, pattern papers for the Curwen Press, book jackets, fabrics and the first greetings telegram for the GPO. Partially paralysed after a stroke at seventy-four, she then became a skilled embroiderer.
4 posters, 5 panel posters, 1928–35. Pages 71, 75

EDWARD McKNIGHT KAUFFER, HON. RDI
1890–1954
Born in Montana, USA, he became an assistant scene painter at Evansville Grand Opera House (c. 1903), going on to study art at the Mark Hopkins Institute in San Francisco. He studied in Paris in 1913, sponsored by Prof. McKnight of the University of Utah, in homage to whom he adopted his middle name. He settled in London in 1914, and Frank Pick gave him his first commission the following year; he became the London Underground's major poster artist and they his main clients. In 1921, he gave up painting entirely in favour of commercial art. While he also produced theatre, costume and exhibition designs, interior and mural decorations, book illustrations, carpets and textiles, it was his posters that proved most influential. The artist PAUL NASH, writing in 1935, considered Kauffer 'responsible above anyone else for the change in attitude towards commercial art in this country'. He returned to America in 1940, to live and work in New York City. Retrospective exhibitions were organized by the Museum of Modern Art, New York (1937) and the Victoria and Albert Museum, London (1955).
94 posters, over 40 panel posters 1915–39. Pages 36, 48, 60, 68, 69

ERIC HENRI KENNINGTON, RA 1888–1960
Born in London, son of painter T. E. Kennington, he studied at Lambeth School of Art (1905–7) and the City and Guilds School. Primarily a portrait painter, he exhibited at the Royal Academy and the Leicester Galleries from 1908. After five months' travel with T. E. Lawrence in the Middle East, he took up sculpture.
6 posters, 1944. Page 102

WILLIAM KERMODE
Studied at Grosvenor School of Modern Art under Iain Macnab, then worked as a book and commercial illustrator, often using wood or lino cutting.
1 poster, 1924. Page 46

R.B. KITAJ, RA b. 1932
Born in Cleveland, Ohio, USA, he worked as a seaman before training as an artist at Cooper Union in New

York. After service in the US Army he came to England to study at the Ruskin School in Oxford and at the Royal College of Art, where his innovative and unconventional work influenced DAVID HOCKNEY. He held his first solo exhibition in Los Angeles in 1963. After teaching in London he became a Guest Professor at the University of California, Berkeley. He has had major exhibitions at the Hayward Gallery in 1976 and the Tate Gallery in 1994. Kitaj married the American painter SANDRA FISHER in 1983.
1 poster, 1993. Page 140

LAURA KNIGHT, RA 1877–1970
Born Laura Johnson at Long Eaton, Derbyshire, she studied at Nottingham School of Art from 1892, where she met the painter Harold Knight whom she married in 1903. Until 1907, they spent much time in Holland, then moved to Cornwall and finally to London. She exhibited at the Royal Academy from 1903, and became the first woman Academician in 1936. Best known for her studies of the ballet, the circus and gypsies, she also painted landscapes and figures, and during the 1930s designed table- and glassware for Wedgwood, Stuart Crystal and others. A retrospective exhibition of her work was held at the Royal Academy in 1965.
7 posters, 1921–57. Page 50

MARY KOOP
Born Mary Bredall, she studied at the Croydon School of Art and the London School of Art under J. M. Swan and FRANK BRANGWYN. She exhibited three times at the Royal Academy.
1 poster, 1925. Page 60

LUCAS KUYS b. 1942
Born in Holland, he studied at Rotterdam Academy of Art. He became an influential artist in the Netherlands where he was secretary to Amsterdam's oldest society for practicing artists and lectured at the city's Rietveld Academy of Art. He later moved to Norfolk, creating a studio in a houseboat on the coast.
1 poster, 1992. Page 138

EDWARD PURSER LANCASTER 1911–54
Born in Southport, he studied at Southport, Liverpool and Chelsea Schools of Art and became a painter and mural artist.
3 posters, 1939–48. Page 90

MARC LAURENCE
1 poster, 1912. Page 19

BILL LEESON
2 posters, 1966–7. Page 122

ALFRED LEETE 1882–1933
Born in Thorpe Abchurch, Northampton, the son of a farmer, he had no formal art training. He became a humorous illustrator, contributing cartoons to magazines as well as illustrating books, including *The Worries of Wilhelm*, published in 1916. His Lord Kitchener poster 'Your Country Needs You' (1914) is the best known war poster of all time and has inspired many adaptations.
4 posters, 2 panel posters, 1915–28. Page 55

THOMAS ENOCH LIGHTFOOT
A watercolour painter who lived in Bedford Park,

London. He exhibited at the Royal Academy in 1930 and 1931.
1 poster, 1932. Page 46

STANISLAUS S. LONGLEY 1894–1966
Born in Aylesbury, Buckinghamshire, he studied at the Regent Street Polytechnic and became a decorative figure work artist and landscape painter.
8 panel posters, 1927–33. Pages 55, 59

LOWES DALBAC LUARD d. 1944
Oil and watercolour painter.
1 poster, 1943. Page 104

BRUCE MCLEAN b. 1944
Born in Glasgow, he studied at Glasgow School of Art (1961–3), then at St Martin's School of Art, London (1963–6), on an advanced sculpture course. During the second half of the 1960s he produced a number of experimental works characterized by impermanence, including 'floating sculpture' and performance art. In the mid-1970s he began to paint, initially as preparation for performance works. He has had major retrospectives of his work at the Museum of Modern Art, Oxford (1975), the Third Eye Centre, Glasgow (1980), and the Whitechapel Art Gallery, London (1983), the latter subsequently shown in Berlin.
1 poster, 1989. Page 129

MANNER
1 poster, 1929. Page 61

ANDRÉ EDOUARD MARTY 1882–1974
Born in Paris, he studied at the Ecole des Beaux Arts and worked as an illustrator, engraver and theatre designer. He is particularly known for fashion plates produced for the *Gazette du Bon Ton* and *Vogue*. He also illustrated de luxe editions of French books, fashionable during the 1920s.
4 posters, 13 panel posters, 1931–3. Page 51

ENID CRYSTAL DOROTHY MARX, RDI 1902–98
Born in London, she studied at the Central School of Arts and Crafts and the Royal College of Art. Painter, printmaker, children's book illustrator, designer of book jackets, trademarks and postage stamps, she initially made a living designing textiles, first with Barren and Larcher (1925–7), then in her own studio. Frank Pick commissioned designs for woollen moquette seating fabric for Underground trains from her in 1937. She was a member of the Design Panel of the Utility Furniture Advisory Committee (1944–7), the first woman engraver to be appointed a Royal Designer for Industry (1944), and was elected a Fellow of the Society of Industrial Artists.
3 posters, 1957–64. Page 112

ROBERT FLAVELL MICKLEWRIGHT b. 1923
Born in Staffordshire, he studied at Croydon School of Art (1939), Wimbledon School of Art (1947–9) and the Slade (1949–52), and now practises as a freelance painter, designer and illustrator.
3 posters, 1968–75. Page 123

JOHN MILLER b. 1931
Born in London, he was trained as an architect. In 1958

he moved to Cornwall and joined the Newlyn Society of Artists in 1961. He had a retrospective exhibition at Newlyn Orion Gallery in 1978 and since 1982 has exhibited with the David Messom Gallery.
1 poster, 2000. Page 153

FRED MILLETT
2 posters, 1962–8. Page 116

FRANCIS JOHN MINTON 1917–57
Born near Cambridge, he studied at the St John's Wood School of Art (1935–8), then lived in France. He taught at the Camberwell School of Art (1943–7), the Central School of Arts and Crafts (1947–8), and the Royal College of Art (1948–57). Minton's work as a painter, under the banner of 'British Neo-Romanticism', was much discussed in post-war Britain and made him a very influential teacher. The Arts Council organized a memorial exhibition of his work in 1958, and Reading Museum and Art Gallery staged a retrospective in 1974.
1 poster, 1951. Page 113

LÁSZLÓ MOHOLY-NAGY 1895–1946
Born in Hungary, he studied law in Budapest. Taking up painting and photography after the First World War, he was in close contact with revolutionary, avant garde artists in Budapest before moving to Berlin in 1920. He taught at the Bauhaus from 1923 to 1928, as head of the Preliminary Course in design, and in the Metal Workshop. An artist engineer, he co-edited the fourteen Bauhaus books, while privately working on experimental photography and documentary films. From 1928–33 he worked in Berlin principally as a stage designer, then moved to Amsterdam. He arrived in England in 1935 and met with considerable success as a commercial, graphic and exhibition designer. One-man exhibitions were held at the London Gallery and the Royal Photographic Society, before he left for the USA; he was Director of the New Bauhaus in Chicago from 1937. In 1939, he founded the Chicago School of Design.
3 posters, 1936–7. Page 85

MOLLY MOSS
Born in Hull, Yorkshire, she attended the general course at Hull Art School in 1931, then showed her work at a number of mixed exhibitions in London. She was a member of the Hampstead Artists' Council.
1 poster, 1950. Page 110

PAUL NASH 1889–1946
Born in London, he studied at Chelsea Polytechnic (1906–7) and the Slade (1910–11), where he met Ben Nicholson. Early recognition as a landscape artist was followed by an invitation from Roger Fry to join the Omega Workshops. Watercolours of the war-torn landscape in France led to a one-man show in London in 1917. A book illustrator and theatre designer, he was tutor in painting at the Royal College of Art (1924–5 and 1938–40), where his pupils included EDWARD BAWDEN and ERIC RAVILIOUS. In close contact with the European avant garde during the 1930s, he was a cofounder and promoter of Unit One (1933), and exhibited with the International Surrealist group in London (1936), as well as major Surrealist shows in Tokyo, Amsterdam and Paris (1937–8). A retrospective exhibition was held at the Tate Gallery in 1975.
3 posters, 1 panel poster, 1935–6. Pages 84, 85

CHRISTOPHER RICHARD WYNNE NEVINSON 1889–1946
Born in Hampstead, London, he studied at St John's Wood School of Art (1907–8), the Slade (1908–12), and in Paris at the Academie Julian (1912–13), where he shared a studio with Modigliani. He exhibited with other Futurists in 1913 and in 1914 co-wrote with Marinetti 'Vital English Art: A Futurist Manifesto'. He had his first one-man show in London in 1916, where he exhibited his Futurist images of war on the Western Front. He later worked in a variety of styles, and refused to become part of any particular movement.
11 posters, 1921–39. Page 64

FRANK ORMROD 1896–1988
He taught at the Slade before becoming a lecturer in design at Reading School of Art (1934–64).
1 poster, 1937. Page 82

PADDEN
1 poster, 1921. Page 44

CHARLES PAINE
He studied at Salford College of Art and the Royal College of Art, then taught at Edinburgh College of Art. His poster designs for London Underground were mainly the result of his association with the Baynard Press.
19 posters, 3 panel posters, 1920–9. Page 67

DOROTHY PATON
1 poster, 9 panel posters, 1927–9. Page 74

JAMES MCINTOSH PATRICK 1907–98
Born in Dundee, he began to etch at the age of fourteen. He studied at Glasgow School of Art (1924–8), and is noted for his detailed Scottish landscape paintings. Frank Pick purchased one in 1937, and commissioned the Harrow Weald poster designs soon afterwards.
2 posters, 1938. Page 91

CHARLES PEARS 1873–1958
Born in Pontefract, Yorkshire, he moved to London in 1897 and became a theatrical caricaturist on *Pick-Me-Up* (1898–1902), later a marine painter and illustrator, and graphic designer.
44 posters, 1913–36. Pages 34, 65, 89

HERRY PERRY d. 1962
Heather Perry was trained at the London County Council's Central School of Arts and Crafts where she specialized in wood carving, though she later earned her living designing posters, pub signs and playing cards; her verse was published in *Punch*.
13 posters, 41 panel posters, 1928–37. Pages 66, 75

ANDREW POWER see SYBIL ANDREWS.

GERALD SPENCER PRYSE 1881–1956
Born in London, he studied art in London and Paris, then worked as a watercolourist, lithographer, engraver and poster designer. During the First World War he served as a captain and Official War Artist, drawing lithographs straight on to stone in the trenches. His paintings were widely exhibited in Britain and abroad.
3 posters, 1913–21. Page 32

TOM PURVIS, RDI 1888–1957
Born in Bristol, the son of a sailor turned marine painter, he trained at Camberwell School of Art as well as with Sickert and Degas. After six years in advertising, he became freelance and designed his first independent poster for Dewar's whisky in 1907. Other major commissions followed, including many posters for the London & North Eastern Railway which are among his best-known works. He served on the committee for the British Art in Industry Exhibition at the Royal Academy (1935) and was made a Royal Designer for Industry in 1936.
2 posters, 5 panel posters 1932–4. Page 73

ERIC WILLIAM RAVILIOUS 1903–42
Born in London, he studied at the Eastbourne School of Art (1919–22), then the Design School at the Royal College of Art (1922–5) where PAUL NASH was his tutor. He designed wood engravings for book illustrations, as well as book jackets, and jointly with EDWARD BAWDEN and Cyril Mahoney painted the murals for Morley College, London (1928–30). A design tutor at the Royal College of Art (1930–8), he worked on porcelain, glass, furniture and textile designs; in 1937, he executed the wall decoration for the British Pavilion at the Paris Exhibition. During the late 1930s, he increasingly turned to watercolour painting and colour lithography. The Crafts Council organized a major exhibition of his work in 1986.
2 poster artworks, c. 1935. Page 88

MAN RAY 1890–1976
Born Emmanuel Rudnitzky in Philadelphia, he studied at the New York National Academy of Design (1908) and at the Ferrer School (191 –13), where he became friends with the photographer Alfred Stieglitz. In 1915, the year of his first exhibition, he met Marcel Duchamp and began experimenting with photography. He went to live in France in 1921 and the following year created his first photograms (which he called 'rayographs'): images made without a camera by exposing objects directly on light-sensitive paper. His first album of rayographs, Les Champs Delicieux, was introduced by his fellow Dadaist Tristan Tzara. Deeply involved in Surrealism, he was a fashion photographer (particularly for Paul Poiret), a portraitist and an experimental film maker. He spent the years 1940 to 1951 in Hollywood, painting and teaching photography at the Art Center School. In 1972 the Musée National d'Art Moderne in Paris held a retrospective exhibition of his work.
1 poster, 1939. Page 77

AGNES RICHARDSON 1885–1951
Born in Wimbledon, the daughter of a printer, she studied at Lambeth School of Art and became a popular illustrator of children's stories, annuals and picture postcards.
3 posters, 1912–22. Page 35

PETER ROBERSON b. 1907
Born in Oxford, he was awarded a scholarship to Oxford Art School where he spent three years, eventually specializing in lettering and illumination. Employed at the Clarendon Press from 1924, he mostly drew maps, but also designed book jackets. He moved to London in 1935 and worked in advertising as a visualizer, illustrator, poster designer and copywriter.
29 posters, 5 panel posters, 1951–78. Page 109

ESMÉ ROBERTS b. c. 1913
She ran her own studio and designed book jackets.
2 posters, 1934–5. Page 89

PHILIP ROBERTS
1 poster, 1960. Page 115

WILLIAM ROBERTS, RA 1895–1980
Born in Hackney, East London the son of a carpenter, he studied at St Martin's School of Art while apprenticed to an advertising firm. He attended the Slade (1910–13), and became interested in Cubism before joining the Vorticists in 1914. He taught at the Central School of Arts and Crafts from 1925 to 1930 and exhibited at the Royal Academy from 1945 until his death. The Tate Gallery held a major retrospective exhibition of his work in 1965.
1 poster, 1 panel poster, 1951–3. Page 111

ALAN ROGERS
2 posters, 1930. Page 89

RUTH SANDYS
1 poster, 1925. Page 67

TONY SARG b. 1830
Painter, illustrator and caricaturist, born in Guatemala.
30 posters 8 panel posters, 1912–1 . Page 26

HANS SCHLEGER, RDI 1898–1976
'Zero' was born in Germany, and studied at the National School of Applied Art in Berlin during the early 1920s, at the time when the Bauhaus was making an impact. From 1924–9 he lived in New York, working first as a freelance graphic designer, then as art director for an advertising agency. He settled in London in 1932 where he opened his own studio. During the 1930s he designed numerous posters and was a close friend of MCKNIGHT KAUFFER. An early proponent of the concept of 'corporate identity', he designed the bus-stop symbols for London Transport in 1935. Major commissions included the symbols for the Design Centre in Haymarket, London (1955) and the Edinburgh International Festival (1966, replaced 1978), as well as the creation of a unified design policy for a number of British companies. He lectured widely and was a visiting associate professor at the Institute of Design, Chicago, for a year. He was made a Royal Designer for Industry in 1959.
31 posters 12 panel posters, 1935–7. Page 76

EBERHARD SCHULZE
A mosaicist, he worked in conjunction with HANS UNGER.
3 posters, 1962–70. Page 127

GEOFF SENIOR
Commissioned via FCB Advertising Agency.
1 poster, 1977. Page 136

MARC FERNAND SEVERIN b. 1906
Born in Brussels, the son of a poet, he studied philosophy and letters, then art and archaeology at Ghent University. He lived in England 1932–40 and 1945–9, first working as art director of R. C. Casson advertising agency, then as a freelance artist, advertising designer and book illustrator. He taught at the Institut Supérieur des Beaux Arts, Antwerp (1949–72) and the

Institut des Hautes Etudes Typographiques Plantin, Belgium (from 1956).
4 posters, 1938. Page 93

CHARLES SHARLAND
A prolific studio artist at Waterlow Printers.
36 posters, 1908–22. Pages 25, 27

NANCY SMITH 1882–c.1965
Born in Chesterfield, Derbyshire, she was art school trained and illustrated a number of children's books in 1909– 4 including Harrap editions of Robinson Crusoe and Hiawatha.
4 posters, 8 panel posters 1915–22 Page 35

RICHARD SPICE b.1965
Born in Dartford, Kent he trained at Trent Polytechnic, graduating with a fine art degree in 1987. He started his career as an illustrator with a commission from the Body Shop for a window poster. Subsequent commissions included work for Barclays Bank, the Royal Festival Hall and Benson & Hedges. His editorial work as an illustrator has included Vogue, Elle, Essentials and the Observer Magazine as clients. He now works as a graphic designer in Nottingham for greetings card company Paper Rose.
1 poster 1991. Page 143

WALTER E. SPRADBERY 1889–1969
Born in East Dulwich, London, he studied at Walthamstow Art School, then worked as an art teacher. He regularly exhibited at the Royal Academy, and worked as a watercolourist and poster designer.
52 posters, 18 panels, 1912–44. Pages 26, 90, 96, 97

HARRY STEVENS b. 1919
Born in Manchester, he studied privately and became a freelance designer. He joined the Society of Industrial Artists in 1955 and was elected a Fellow ten years later. He has specialized in poster design for a wide variety of clients and agencies.
11 posters, 1 panel poster, 1960–74. Pages 119, 123

GRAHAM SUTHERLAND 1903–80
Born in London, he became an engineering apprentice for the Midland Railway at Derby in 1919, but then enrolled at Goldsmith's College of Art where he specialized in etching (1921–6). He exhibited at the Royal Academy from 1923 to 1929. He then turned to commercial work, designing glassware, ceramics, postage stamps and especially posters, as well as painting, notably portraits. He exhibited with the Surrealist Group in London (1936), and had one-man shows in 1938 and 1940; in 1962 he designed the tapestry 'Christ in Glory' for Coventry Cathedral. Retrospective exhibitions have been held at the Institute of Contemporary Arts (1951) and The Tate Gallery (1953 and 1982).
7 posters, 1933–6. Pages 84, 91

BETTY SWANWICK, RA, RWS 1915–89
Born in London, she studied at Goldsmith's College School of Art, the Royal College of Art and the Central School of Arts and Crafts. She was a tutor at Goldsmith's College 1948–69, a book illustrator, painter, designer and muralist.
9 posters, 2 panel posters, 1936–54. Page 112

159

FRED TAYLOR 1875–1963

Born n London, he studied at Goldsmith's College and worked at the Waring and Gillow Studio. A leading poster artist from 1908 to the 1940s with regular commissions from railway and shipping companies, he exhibited at the Royal Academy, and was also a decorative painter.

62 posters, 31 panel posters, 1908–46. Pages 29, 39, 47, 98, 99

HORACE TAYLOR 1881–1934

Born n London, he studied at the Camden School of Art, the Royal Academy Schools in London and the Roya Academy, Munich. A painter and poster and stage designer, he worked as a cartoonist for the Manchester *Guardian* but from 1922 was engaged almost entirely on commercial art.

4 posters, 1924–6. Pages 58, 70, 71

JULIAN TREVELYAN, RA 1910–88

He studied at Cambridge, where he ran a gallery with Humphrey Jennings before deciding to become a painter. He studied in Paris at Stanley William Hayter's Atelier 17, as well as with Léger and Ozenfant (1931–4). On his return to London, he continued experimental work, and participated in the Surrealism Exhibition (1936). During 1938, he painted and photographed for Mass Observation. He taught at the Chelsea School of Art (1950–60) and was tutor in etching at the Royal College of Art (1955–63). He wrote three books: *Indigo Days* (1958), *The Artist and his World* (1961) and *Etching* (1963).

poster, 1988. Page 131

LYNN TRICKETT b. 1945

Trained at Chelsea School of Art. Met BRIAN WEBB whilst working at the Derek Forsyth Partnership in London in 1970, and together they formed the Trickett & Webb partnership in 1971. Their practice specializes in graphic design packaging and exhibition design.

2 posters, 1993–99. Page 147

JENNIE TUFFS b. 1943

Born in London, she studied at St Martin's School of Art (1961–6), the Accademia dei Belli Arti, Florence (1963–4), and Goldsmith's College (1966–7). She has worked as an art teacher, clothes designer and lecturer. In 1979 she began painting natural forms and has had a number of solo shows, principally in Scotland, but also including an exhibition at the Royal Botanic Gardens, Kew, in 1989.

7 posters, 1987–97. Pages 133, 139

SUE TURNER

Commissioned via The Fine White Line Design agency.
1 poster, 1990. Page 145

HANS UNGER 1915–75

Born in Germany, he studied poster design in the studio of Jupp Wiertz in Berlin (1934–5) before emigrating to South Africa, where he worked as a freelance commercial designer in Cape Town. He settled in London in 1948.

42 posters, 20 panel posters, 1950–74. Pages 114, 119, 127

EDWARD ALEXANDER WADSWORTH 1889–1949

Born in Cleckheaton, Yorkshire, he studied engineering in Munich (1906–7), then at Bradford School of Art and the Slade (1907–12). He was a signatory of the Vorticist Manifesto in 1914, and worked as a 'dazzle' camouflage artist during the First World War. Later he worked as a painter, often of marine subjects, as well as a print-maker and book illustrator; his woodcuts made a particular impact at a time when wood engraving was just being revived.

3 posters, 1 panel poster, 1936. Page 88

WARBIS BROTHERS

1 poster, 1915. Page 33

PAUL WEARING b. 1959

Born in Bulawayo, Zimbabwe, he studied at the Royal College of Art, London. Since graduating in 1983 he has worked with major publishers and retailers world wide. His commercial work has covered a varied range of illustration including brand development, corporate literature, publishing, editorial, packaging, retail display, advertising and fashion graphics.

1 poster, 1999. Page 149

BRIAN WEBB b. 1945

Trained at Canterbury College of Art. Formed the Trickett & Webb partnership with LYNN TRICKETT in 1971. Their practice specializes in graphic design (including posters and stamps), packaging and exhibition design and has won a number of design awards.

2 posters, 1993–99. Page 147

SYDNEY THOMAS COOPER WEEKS b. 1878

Born in Blackheath, London.
5 posters, 4 panel posters, 1911–13. Page 26

J. WALTER WEST 1860–1933

A painter, lithographer and designer, he studied at St John's Wood School of Art, the Royal Academy Schools and in Paris.
7 posters, 1916–17. Page 39

KIM WHEATER

Commissioned via FCB Advertising agency,
1 poster, 1984. Page 126

REX JOHN WHISTLER 1905–44

Born in Eltham, Kent, he attended the Royal Academy Schools from the age of fifteen, then went on to study at the Slade (1922–6). His murals for the Tate Gallery Refreshment Room (1928) made him one of the most fashionable artists of his time. During the 1930s he worked as a stage and costume designer on theatre and opera productions, including *Fidelio* at Covent Garden (1934), and became a prolific book illustrator.

2 posters, 1928. Page 49

HAROLD SANDYS WILLIAMSON 1892–1978

Born in Leeds, he studied at the Leeds School of Art then the Royal Academy Schools (19 1–14). He produced commercial work for a number of organizations, as well as for the Council for the Encouragement of Music and the Arts (forerunner of the Arts Council), formed in 1945. He was Headmaster of Chelsea Polytechnic 1930–58.

16 posters, 1 panel poster, 1924–39. Page 65

VERA WILLOUGHBY 1870–1939

She studied at the Slade School of Fine Art under Legros. Initially a watercolour artist, she became a successful book illustrator in the late 920s, and also worked as a commercial and costume designer.

4 posters, 7 panel posters, 1928–35. Page 63

F. C. WITNEY

1 poster, 1913. Page 23

TOM WOOD b. 1955

Born in Dar es Salaam, Tanganyika, he moved with his family to West Yorkshire in 1959. Wood studied at the Batley School of Art (1975), Leeds Polytechnic (1976) and Sheffield School of Art (1976–8). He has had several solo exhibitions, including one at the Dean Clough Contemporary Art Gallery, Halifax, in 1989, which was devoted to his commissioned portrait of H.R.H. The Prince of Wales.

1 poster, 1989. Page 137

ANNA KATRINA ZINKEISEN, RDI 1901–76

Born in Kilcreggan, Scotland, she studied at the Royal Academy Schools in 1916. Principally a painter of society portraits and flowers, she also executed murals (including commissions for the liners *Queen Mary* and *Queen Elizabeth*), made sculpture, designed book jackets and magazine posters. Her sister Doris, well known as a theatrical set designer, also designed posters for London Transport. She was made a Royal Designer for Industry in 1940.

4 posters, 16 panel posters, 1933–4. Page 83